ASEXUAL PEOPLE

Books LLC®, Wiki Series, Memphis, USA, 2011. ISBN: 9781155827421. www.booksllc.net
Copyright: http://creativecommons.org/licenses/by-sa/3.0/deed.en

Table of Contents

Ann Lee 1	Emilie Autumn 6	Morrissey 17
Bradford Cox 2	J. M. Barrie 10	Paula Poundstone 25
David Jay 4	Janeane Garofalo 13	T. E. Lawrence 26
Edward Gorey 4	Keri Hulme 17	Tim Gunn 32

Introduction

Purchase of this book entitles you to a free trial membership in the publisher's book club at www.booksllc.net. (Time limited offer.) Simply enter the barcode number from the back cover onto the membership form. The book club entitles you to select from hundreds of thousands of books at no additional charge. You can also download a digital copy of this and related books to read on the go. Simply enter the title or subject onto the search form to find them.

Each chapter in this book ends with a URL to a hyperlinked online version. Type the URL exactly as it appears. If you change the URL's capitalization it won't work. Use the online version to access related pages, websites, footnotes, tables, color photos, updates. Click the version history tab to see the chapter's contributors. Click the edit link to suggest changes.

A large and diverse editor base collaboratively wrote the book, not a single author. After a long process of discussion and debate, the chapters gradually took on a neutral point of view reached through consensus. Additional editors expanded and contributed to chapters striving to achieve balance and comprehensive coverage. This reduced the regional or cultural bias found in many other books and provided access and breadth on subject matter otherwise little documented.

Ann Lee

Mother **Ann Lee** (29 February 1736 – 8 September 1784) was the leader of the United Society of Believers in Christ's Second Appearing, or Shakers.

In 1774 she and a small group of her followers emigrated from England to New York. After several years, they gathered at Niskayuna, renting land from the Manor of Rensselaerswyck, Albany County, New York (the area now called Colonie). They worshiped by ecstatic dancing or "shaking", which dubbed them as the Shaking Quakers, or Shakers. Ann Lee preached to the public and led the Shaker church at a time when few women did either.

Ann Lee was born in Manchester, England, and baptised privately at Manchester Cathedral on 1 June 1742, aged 6.

Ann Lee's father, John Lees, was a blacksmith during the day and a tailor at night. It is probable that Ann Lee's original surname was Lees, but somewhere through time it changed to Lee. Little is known about her mother other than she was a very religious woman. When Ann was young she worked in a cotton factory, then she worked as a cutter of hatter's fur, and later as a cook in a Manchester infirmary.

Beginning during her youth, Ann Lee was uncomfortable with sexuality, especially her own. This repulsion towards sexual activity continued and manifested itself most poignantly in her repeated attempts to avoid marriage and remain single. Eventually her father forced her to marry Abraham Standley. They were married at Manchester Cathedral on 5 January 1761. She became pregnant eight times, experiencing four stillbirths and four living children, none of whom lived past the age of 6. Her difficult pregnancies and the loss of eight children were traumatic experiences that contributed to Ann Lee's dislike of sexual relations. Lee developed radical religious convictions that advocated celibacy and the abandonment of marriage, as well as the importance of pursuing perfection in every facet of life. She differed from the Quakers, who, though they supported gender equality, did not accept forbidding sexuality within marriage.

In 1758 she joined the Wardleys, an English sect founded by Jane and preacher James Wardley; this was the precursor to the Shaker sect. She believed in and taught her followers that it is possible to attain perfect holiness by giving up sexual relations. Like her predecessors, the Wardleys, she taught that the shaking and trembling were caused by sin being purged from the body by the power of the Holy Spirit, purifying the worshiper.

Rise to Prominence

In England, Ann Lee rose to prominence by urging other believers to preach more publicly concerning the imminent second coming, and to attack sin more boldly and unconventionally. She spoke of visions and messages from God, claiming that she had received a vision from God the message that celibacy and confession of sin are the only true road to salvation, the only way in which the Kingdom of God could be established on the earth. She was frequently imprisoned for breaking the Sabbath by dancing and shouting, and for blasphemy.

Lee often was characterized as a virago (a woman with masculine, domineering attributes), possibly because most English and Americans could not accept her ideals of gender equality, or possibly because she was extraordinarily outspoken.

She claimed to have had many miraculous escapes from death. She told of being examined by four clergymen of the Established Church, she spoke to them for four hours in 72 tongues.

While in prison in Manchester for 14 days, she said she had a revelation that "a complete cross against the lusts of generation, added to a full and explicit confession, before witnesses, of all the sins committed under its influence, was the only possible remedy and means of salvation." After this, probably in 1770, she was chosen by the Society as "Mother in spiritual things" and called herself "Ann, the Word" and also "Mother Ann." After being released from prison a second time, witnesses say Mother Ann performed a number of miracles, including healing the sick.

Ann Lee eventually decided to leave England for America in order to escape the persecution (i.e. multiple arrests and stays in prison) she experienced in the hostile religious climate of the United Kingdom.

Move to America

In 1774 a revelation led her to take a select band to America. She was accompanied by her husband, who soon afterwards deserted her. Also following her to America was her brother, William Lee (1740–1784); Nancy Lee, her niece; James Whittaker (1751–1787), who had been brought up by Mother Ann and was probably related to her; John Hocknell (1723–1799), who provided the funds for the trip; his son, Richard; and James Shepherd and Mary Partington. Mother Ann arrived on August 6, 1774, in New York City. Here they stayed for nearly 5 years. In 1776 Hocknell bought land at Niskayuna, in the township of Watervliet, near Albany, and the Shakers settled there, where a unique community life began to develop and thrive.

Ann Lee recognized how revolutionary her ideas were when she said, "We [the Shakers] are the people who turned the world upside down." Lee was also neutral during the American Revolution. Maintaining the position that they were pacifists, Ann Lee and her followers did not side with either the British or the colonists.

Beginning in the spring of 1781 Mother Ann and some of her followers went on an extensive missionary journey to find converts in Massachusetts and Connecticut. They often stayed in the homes of local sympathizers, such as the Benjamin Osborn House near the New York - Massachusetts line. There were also songs attributed to her which were sung without words.

The followers of Mother Ann came to believe that she embodied all the perfections of God in female form. The fact that Ann Lee considered herself to be Christ's female counterpart was unique. She preached that sinfulness could be avoided by not only treating men and women equally, but also by keeping them separated so as to prevent any sort of temptation leading to impure acts. Celibacy and confession of sin were essential for salvation. Ann Lee was a gifted evangelist and marketed her message effectively.

Ann Lee's mission throughout New England was especially successful in converting groups who were already outside of the mainstream of New England Protestantism, including followers of Shadrack Ireland. However, the Shakers were sometimes met by violent mobs, such as in Shirley, Massachusetts, and Ann Lee suffered violence at their hands more than once. Because of these hardships Mother Ann became quite frail; she died on September 8, 1784, at the age of 48. She died at Watervliet and is buried in the Shaker cemetery located in the Watervliet Shaker Historic District.

Shakers in New Lebanon, New York, experienced a 10-year period of revelations in 1837 called the Era of Manifestations. It was also referred to as *Mother Ann's Work*.

Source (edited): "http://en.wikipedia.org/wiki/Ann_Lee"

Bradford Cox

Bradford James Cox (born May 15, 1982) is an American musician best known as the lead singer and guitarist of Atlanta, Georgia-based psychedelic and ambient band Deerhunter. He also pursues a solo career under the moniker **Atlas Sound**. Cox formed Deerhunter with drummer Moses Archuleta in 2001. The band has released 5 LPs along with several singles and EPs. Atlas Sound is a name Cox has used since he was ten to refer to his own music, but his first full-length produced under the name was *Let the Blind Lead Those Who Can See but Cannot Feel*, released in 2008. Cox's method of creating music is stream-of-consciousness, and he does not write lyrics in advance.

Musical career

Deerhunter

Cox founded Deerhunter with bassist Paul Harper and drummer Dan Walton (who named the band) in early 2001.

The band expanded after Cox met a teenage transient, Moses Archuleta, who was sleeping on the floor of Cox's friends. Archuleta initially played Acetone Organ and electronics. The band's first shows were experimental and based on improvisation. Cox continued recording slightly more structured material and releasing it on CD-R and cassette using the name Atlas Sound. Paul Harper moved to Ohio and was replaced by Justin Bosworth. At this point Colin Mee also joined the band on guitar. Dan Walton left and Cox suggested Archuleta move to drums. The band's live shows and recordings became more song-oriented. They recorded their debut 7" for Die Slaughterhaus. Josh Fauver joined the band in 2004 after Bosworth died in a freak skateboarding accident. This lineup recorded Deerhunter's debut LP on Atlanta label Stickfigure. Cox suggested Lockett Pundt, who he befriended while attending Harrison High School join the band on guitar so that he could concentrate on vocals and electronics. This lineup recorded their breakthrough record, 2007's Cryptograms. Colin Mee left the band after failing to show up for a North American tour. The band are now a four piece consisting of Cox on guitar and vocals, Pundt on guitar and occasional vocals, Fauver on bass, and Archuleta on drums.

Atlas Sound

"Atlas Sound" is the musical solo project of Cox, although he has used the name to represent his music since he was a child. He had access to a cassette player with two tape decks, which he used to layer guitar and drum sounds, and his own voice. In listening to some of these old tapes (of which Cox believes he has over five hundred in storage) he found "Some of it is absolutely, terrifyingly bad, but sometimes I'm just like, 'Wow, that's cool.' That's actually how some Deerhunter songs happened. 'Spring Hall Convert' [from *Cryptograms*] was like that. That was a tape I made in ninth or tenth grade." Cox writes his music stream-of-consciousness, not writing lyrics in advance, and constructing songs by adding more parts until he feels "it's getting crowded." The name of his project is derived from the brand of tape player he used, Atlas Sound.

Cox began Atlas Sound in the wake of his work with Deerhunter because "I have ideas that I can't make work with a five piece rock band...There's kind of this palette of sounds that I use that I don't necessarily get to use with Deerhunter." Because the music Deerhunter makes is a collaborative effort, Cox does not want to assert himself as its principal songwriter. "I might have an idea for a fragment of a song, but I want to leave it skeletal so the guys can fill it out. Whereas with Atlas Sound, everything is done in an hour." Cox created the music for his first record in the software Ableton Live, utilizing an array of computer-based instruments, as well as his own live recordings.

To date, there have been six full-length releases by Cox as Atlas Sound: *Let the Blind Lead Those Who Can See but Cannot Feel* in 2008, *Logos* in 2009, and Bedroom Databank in 2010, which is separated into four different albums. The lyrics of *Let the Blind Lead* are autobiographical in nature, reflecting life experiences of Cox. In discussing his second album, Cox characterized his first as being a "bedroom laptop type thing" and "Very introverted." In contrast, *Logos* was written in several parts of the world, and is "not about me. There are collaborations with other musicians. The lyrics are not autobiographical. The view is a lot more panoramic and less close-up. I became bored with introspection." An unfinished version of *Logos* was leaked onto the internet in August 2008, over a year before its release date. In response, Cox almost ceased production on the record, later saying "I did not react well to the leak, in retrospect. It became the kind of internet-fueled drama that I was quickly learning to despise."

In late 2010, Cox published four volumes of demos on his blog, entitled "Bedroom Databank". These demos were taken down from Mediafire by Sony, but they later apologized to Cox, stating that they "were mistakenly removed". Atlas Sound has been chosen by Animal Collective to perform at the All Tomorrow's Parties festival that they curated in May 2011.

Other work

Cox has also recorded as part of other bands, such as the short lived "Wet Dreams", an otherwise all-girl garage / noise band in which he played drums. He also recorded several tracks on the Black Lips second album *We Did Not Know the Forest Spirit Made the Flowers Grow*, playing drums on the song "Notown Blues" from that album. Regarding this album, Bradford said in an interview: "People look at what's successful, and what's successful is what's easy on the ears, things that aren't challenging," he says. "Nobody wants to listen to something that sounds awkward and makes you cringe because it's real personal or idiosyncratic. People just want to hear things that sounds familiar already to them. I make really accessible pop stuff, but at the same time I have no problem making something creepy or just odd."

Cox contributed to the Karen O-scored soundtrack for the 2009 film *Where the Wild Things Are*.

Equipment

Guitars

For the most part, Bradford favors vintage and modern Fender and Gibson guitars. Some of his guitars include:

- Fender Jaguar (1966 Sunburst with bound neck)
- Fender Jazzmaster (1964 Originally white, now yellow)
- Fender Stratocaster
- '74 Gibson Les Paul Signature
- Fender Bronco (70s stripped natural finish)

Effects & amplifiers

Pedalboard

- Boss TU-2 Chromatic Tuner
- Line 6 DL4
- Home Brew Electronics Power Screamer
- Eventide PitchFactor
- Behringer Reverb Machine RV600
- Ibanez DE7

- Digitech DigiVerb (through Mic for Vocals)
- Digitech DigiDelay (through Mic for Vocals)
- MXR Distortion +
- Z.Vex Box of Rock
- Boss SL-20 Slicer
- Boss DS-1
- Boss SD-1

(this list in incomplete)

Amps

When playing with Deerhunter, Bradford will usually run his guitars through a Vox AC30 amplifier, and occasionally a Marshall half-stack or a Fender Hot Rod DeVille 410.

Songwriting

Cox describes his mode of songwriting as 'automatic or stream-of-consciousness'. "Usually I go into a sort of trance and I'll have five or six songs afterwards", he said, speaking to Victoria Segal of *Q* in November 2010. "What is interesting is seeing how the band adapts them and mutates them into the final product. Lots of accidents and primitive irrational things happen. It can be difficult trying to explain the process to a producer or engineer. They generally want to help you polish things and I tend to want to sabotage that", he added.

Personal life

Cox was born with the genetic disorder Marfan syndrome. As a teenager, he dropped out of high school (although later earned a GED) and his parents divorced, leaving him "to live in my childhood home alone. I literally lived in this large suburban house by myself." Cox has called his changing music taste growing up reflective of his life and mental state. Around the age of ten, Cox's disorder began to affect his body in more visible ways; this is the point at which he "first started looking awkward." With no friends, Cox became interested in how music could sound "heartbreaking or nostalgic or melancholy"; he identified with the title character of the film *Edward Scissorhands*, and especially enjoyed the soundtrack, which was composed by Danny Elfman. Cox's tastes shifted to music that was more "monotonous or hypnotic", such as the Stereolab album *Transient Random-Noise Bursts with Announcements*. Around twenty years of age, his life situation brought about "a period", during which he became "only interested in this certain sort of suburban psychedelic pastoral thing. It was escapism. I didn't want as much emotional manipulation. It's kind of the opposite of *Edward Scissorhands*." Cox describes himself as gay, though he leads a non-sexual lifestyle.

Discography

With Deerhunter:
- 2005 *Turn It Up Faggot*
- 2007 *Cryptograms*
- 2008 *Microcastle*
- 2008 *Weird Era Cont.*
- 2010 *Halcyon Digest*

As Atlas Sound:
- 2008 *Let the Blind Lead Those Who Can See but Cannot Feel*
- 2009 *Logos*

Source (edited): "http://en.wikipedia.org/wiki/Bradford_Cox"

David Jay

David Jay (born April 24, 1982) is an American asexual activist. Jay is the founder and webmaster of the Asexual Visibility and Education Network (AVEN). While a student at Wesleyan University in Connecticut, Jay came out as asexual and launched AVEN's website. His parents are Daniel Jay and Mary Ann Lazarus, and he has a sister, Laura, who is three years younger, as well as a brother, Michael, who is ten years younger.

AVEN, which Salon.com referred to as the "unofficial online headquarters" of the asexuality movement, is widely recognised as the largest online asexual community. Its two main goals are to create public acceptance and discussion about asexuality and to facilitate the growth of a large online asexual community. AVEN currently has over 28,000 registered members.

Jay is featured heavily in Arts Engine's 2011 documentary *(A)sexual*.

Source (edited): "http://en.wikipedia.org/wiki/David_Jay"

Edward Gorey

Edward St. John Gorey (February 22, 1925 – April 15, 2000) was an American writer and artist noted for his macabre illustrated books.

Early life

Edward St. John Gorey was born in Chicago. His parents, Helen Dunham (née Garvey) and Edward Lee Gorey, divorced in 1936 when he was 11, then remarried in 1952 when he was 27. One of his stepmothers was Corinna Mura (1909–65), a cabaret singer who had a small role in the classic film *Casablanca* as the woman playing the guitar while singing "La Marseillaise" at Rick's Café Américain. His father was briefly a journalist. Gorey's maternal great-grandmother, Helen St. John Garvey, was a popular 19th century greeting card writer and artist, from whom he claimed to have inherited his talents.

Gorey attended a variety of local grade schools and then the Francis W. Parker School. He spent 1944 to 1946 in the Army at Dugway Proving Ground in Utah, and then attended Harvard University from 1946 to 1950, where he studied French and roomed with poet Frank O'Hara.

He frequently stated that his formal art training was "negligible"; Gorey studied art for one semester at the

School of the Art Institute of Chicago in 1943.

Career

From 1953 to 1960, he lived in New York City and worked for the Art Department of Doubleday Anchor, illustrating book covers and in some cases adding illustrations to the text. He illustrated works as diverse as *Dracula* by Bram Stoker, *The War of the Worlds* by H. G. Wells, and *Old Possum's Book of Practical Cats* by T. S. Eliot. In later years he produced cover illustrations and interior artwork for many children's books by John Bellairs, as well as books begun by Bellairs and continued by Brad Strickland after Bellairs' death.

His first independent work, *The Unstrung Harp*, was published in 1953. He also published under pen names that were anagrams of his first and last names, such as Ogdred Weary, Dogear Wryde, Ms. Regera Dowdy, and dozens more. His books also feature the names Eduard Blutig ("Edward Gory"), a German language pun on his own name, and O. Müde (German for O. Weary).

The *New York Times* credits bookstore owner Andreas Brown and his store, the Gotham Book Mart, with launching Gorey's career: "it became the central clearing house for Mr. Gorey, presenting exhibitions of his work in the store's gallery and eventually turning him into an international celebrity."

Gorey's illustrated (and sometimes wordless) books, with their vaguely ominous air and ostensibly Victorian and Edwardian settings, have long had a cult following. Gorey became particularly well-known through his animated introduction to the PBS series *Mystery!* in 1980, as well as his designs for the 1977 Broadway production of *Dracula*, for which he won a Tony Award for Best Costume Design. (He was also nominated for Best Scenic Design.)

Edward Gorey's home on Cape Cod (2006).

Because of the settings and style of Gorey's work, many people have assumed he was British; in fact, he only left the U.S. once, for a visit to the Scottish Hebrides. In later years, he lived year-round in Yarmouth Port, Massachusetts, on Cape Cod, where he wrote and directed numerous evening-length entertainments, often featuring his own papier-mâché puppets, an ensemble known as Le Theatricule Stoique. The first of these productions, *Lost Shoelaces,* premiered in Woods Hole, Massachusetts on August 13, 1987. The last was "The White Canoe: an Opera Seria for Hand Puppets," for which Gorey wrote the libretto, with a score by the composer Daniel Wolf. Based on Thomas Moore's poem "The Lake of the Dismal Swamp," the opera was staged after Gorey's death and directed by his friend, neighbor, and longtime collaborator Carol Verburg, with a puppet stage made by his friends and neighbors the noted set designers Herbert Senn and Helen Pond. In the early 1970s, Gorey wrote an unproduced screenplay for a silent film, *The Black Doll*.

Gorey was noted for his fondness for ballet (for many years, he religiously attended all performances of the New York City Ballet), fur coats, tennis shoes, and cats, of which he had many. All figure prominently in his work. His knowledge of literature and films was unusually extensive, and in his interviews, he named Jane Austen, Agatha Christie, Francis Bacon, George Balanchine, Balthus, Louis Feuillade, Ronald Firbank, Lady Murasaki Shikibu, Robert Musil, Yasujiro Ozu, Anthony Trollope, and Johannes Vermeer as some of his favorite artists. Gorey was also an unashamed pop-culture junkie, avidly following soap operas and TV comedies like *Petticoat Junction* and *Cheers*, and he had particular affection for dark genre series like *Buffy the Vampire Slayer*, *Batman: The Animated Series* and *The X-Files*; he once told an interviewer that he so enjoyed the *Batman* series that it was influencing the visual style of one of his upcoming books. Gorey treated TV commercials as an art form in themselves, even taping his favorites for later study. Gorey was especially fond of movies, and for a time he wrote regular reviews for the *Soho Weekly* under the pseudonym Wardore Edgy.

After Gorey's death, one of his executors, Andreas Brown, turned up a large cache of unpublished work, some completed, some incomplete. Brown described the find as "Ample material for many future books and for plays based on his work."

Personal life

Although Gorey's books were popular with children, he did not associate with children much and had no particular fondness for them. Gorey never married, professed to have little interest in romance, and never discussed any specific romantic relationships in interviews. In the book *The Strange Case of Edward Gorey*, published after Gorey's death, his friend Alexander Theroux reported that when Gorey was pressed on the matter of his sexual orientation, he said that even he was not sure whether he was gay or straight. When asked what his sexual preferences were in an interview, he said,

> " I'm neither one thing nor the other particularly. I am fortunate in that I am apparently reasonably undersexed or something...I've never said that I was gay and I've never said that I wasn't...what I'm trying to say is that I am a person before I am anything else.... "

Edward Gorey agreed in an interview that the "sexlessness" of his novels was a product of his asexuality.

From 1996 to his death in April 2000, the normally reclusive artist was the subject of a direct cinema-style documentary directed by Christopher Seufert. (As of 2011, the film and accompanying book have not been released.) He was interviewed on *Tribute To Edward Gorey*, an hour long community Public-access television cable show produced by artist and friend Joyce Kenney. He contributed his videos and personal thoughts. Edward served as judge in Yarmouth art shows and enjoyed activities at the local cable station, studying computer art and serving as cameraman on many Yarmouth shows. His Cape Cod house is called Elephant House and is the subject of a photography book titled *Elephant House: Or, the Home of Edward Gorey*, with photographs and text by Kevin McDermott. The house is now the Edward Gorey House Museum.

Gorey left the bulk of his estate to a charitable trust benefiting cats and dogs, as well as other species including bats and insects.

Style

Gorey is typically described as an illustrator. His books can be found in the humor and cartoon sections of major bookstores, but books like *The Object Lesson* have earned serious critical respect as works of surrealist art. His experimentations — creating books that were wordless, books that were literally matchbox-sized, pop-up books, books entirely populated by inanimate objects — complicates matters still further. As Gorey told Richard Dyer of *The Boston Globe*, "Ideally, if anything [was] any good, it would be indescribable." Gorey classified his own work as literary nonsense, the genre made most famous by Lewis Carroll and Edward Lear.

In response to being called gothic, he stated, "If you're doing nonsense it has to be rather awful, because there'd be no point. I'm trying to think if there's sunny nonsense. Sunny, funny nonsense for children — oh, how boring, boring, boring. As Schubert said, there is no happy music. And that's true, there really isn't. And there's probably no happy nonsense, either."
Source (edited): "http://en.wikipedia.org/wiki/Edward_Gorey"

Emilie Autumn

Emilie Autumn Liddell (born in Los Angeles, on September 22, 1979), better known by her stage name **Emilie Autumn**, is an American singer-songwriter, poet, and violinist. Autumn draws influence for her music—the style of which she has alternatively labeled as "Victoriandustrial" and glam rock—from plays, novels, and history, particularly the Victorian era. Performing with her all-female backing band The Bloody Crumpets, Autumn incorporates elements of classical music, cabaret, electronica, and glam rock with theatrics, burlesque, and "flamboyant" outfits. Outspoken about bipolar disorder and her experience in a modern-day psychiatric ward, she has written an autobiographical novel, 2010's *The Asylum for Wayward Victorian Girls*.

Growing up in Malibu, California, she began learning the violin at the age of four and left regular school five years later with the goal of becoming a world-class violinist; she practiced eight or nine hours a day and read a wide range of literature. Progressing to writing her own music and poetry, she studied under various teachers and went to Indiana University, which she left over issues regarding the relationship between classical music and the appearance of the performer. Through her own independent label Traitor Records, Autumn debuted with her classical album *On a Day: Music for Violin & Continuo*, followed by the release in 2003 of her supernaturally themed album *Enchant*.

She appeared in singer Courtney Love's backing band on her 2004 *America's Sweetheart* tour and returned to the United States. She released the 2006 album *Opheliac* with the German label Trisol Music Group. In 2007, she released *Laced/Unlaced*; the re-release of *On a Day...* appeared as *Laced* with songs on the electric violin as *Unlaced*. She later left Trisol to join New York-based The End Records in 2009 and release *Opheliac* in the United States, where previously it had only been available as an import. Currently she is working on an album entitled *Fight Like A Girl*.

Life and career

1979–2000: Beginnings

Autumn attributes her ability to write music in her mind to the fact that as a child, she played *Pachelbel's Canon in D* mentally every night to suppress her auditory hallucinations caused by bipolar disorder and sleep.

Emilie Autumn was born in Los Angeles, on September 22, 1979. Autumn grew up in Malibu, California, and according to her, "being surrounded by nature and sea had a lot to do with [her] development as a 'free spirit.'" Her mother worked as a seamstress and is a descendant from the Liddell family. A German circus performer, her father immigrated to America at the age of nine and ran away from home at age fourteen; Autumn claims that he suffered abuse from his father and a "difficult and cruel upbringing". He did not share a close relationship with his daughter. She also has a sister. While not musicians, her family enjoyed various genres of music.

At four years old, she started learning the violin, and later commented: "I remember asking for a violin, but I don't remember knowing what one was. I might have thought it was a kind of pony for all I know, but I don't remember being disappointed." Four years later, Autumn made her musical debut as a solo violinist performing with an orchestra, and won a competition. At the age of nine or ten, she left regular school with the goal of becoming a world-class violinist. On her time at the school, she remarked, "I hated it anyway, what with the status as 'weird,' 'antisocial,' and the physical threats, there seemed to be no reason to go anymore, so I just didn't." She practiced eight or nine hours a day, had lessons, read a wide range of literature, participated in orchestra practice, and was homeschooled. Growing up, she owned a large CD collection of "violin concertos, symphonies, chamber music, opera, and a little jazz". She began writing her own music and poetry at age thirteen or fourteen, though she never planned to sing any of her songs. She studied under various teachers and attended Indiana University in Bloomington, but left after two years there, because she disagreed with the prevailing views on individuality and classical music. She believed that neither the audience nor the original composer would be insulted by the clothing and appearance of the performer.

While convinced that she would only play violin, eighteen-year-old Autumn decided to sing on one of her songs as a way of demonstrating to a major music producer, who wanted to sign her on a label, how it should sound. She became unhappy with the changes done to her songs and decided to break away from the label and create her own independent record label, Traitor Records. Through it, she debuted with her classical album *On a Day: Music for Violin & Continuo*, which she recorded in 1997 when she was seventeen years old; its title refers to the fact that the album took only a day to record. It consists of her performing works for the baroque violin accompanied by friends on the cello, harpsichord, and lute. She considered it "more of a demo despite its length" and released it as "a saleable album" after fans who enjoyed her "rock performances starting asking for a classical album so that they could hear more of the violin." She also debuted with her poetry book *Across The Sky & Other Poems* in 2000, later re-released in 2005 as *Your Sugar Sits Untouched* with a music-accompanied audiobook.

2001–05: *Enchant* and collaborations

In the supernaturally themed album *Enchant*, Autumn drew imagery from faery folklore.

As part of a recording project, Autumn traveled to Chicago, Illinois, in 2001, and decided to stay because she enjoyed the public transportation system and music scene there. She released the 2001 extended play (EP) *Chambermaid* while finishing *Enchant*—she alternatively labeled the musical style on *Chambermaid* as "fantasy rock" and cabaret—and wrote the 2001 charity single "By the Sword" after the events of September 11, 2001. According to her, the song is about strength, not violence; the act of swearing by the sword represents "an unbreakable promise to right a wrong, to stay true." On February 26, 2003, she released her concept album *Enchant*, which spanned multiple musical styles: "new age, pop and trip-hop chamber music". The theme of *Enchant* revolved around the supernatural realm and its effect on the modern-day world. Autumn labeled it as "fantasy rock", which dealt with "dreams and stories and ghosts and faeries who'll bite your head off if you dare to touch them". The faery-themed "Enchant Puzzle" appeared on the artwork of the album; her reward for the person who would solve it consisted of faery-related items. At the same time of *Enchant*'s release, Autumn had several side projects: Convent, a musical group for which she recorded all four voices; Ravensong, "a classical baroque ensemble" that she formed with friends in California; and The Jane Brooks Project, which she dedicated to the real-life, 16th-century Jane Brooks—a woman executed for witchcraft.

On the night of the *Enchant* release party, Autumn learned that Courtney Love had invited her to record an album, *America's Sweetheart*, and embark on the tour to promote it. Contributing violin and vocals, Autumn appeared in Love's backing band The Chelsea—Radio Sloan, Dvin Kirakosian, Samantha Maloney, and Lisa Leveridge—on the 2004 tour. Much of Autumn's violin work did not get released on the album; she commented: "This had to do entirely with new producers taking over the project after our little vacation in France, and carefully discarding all of our sessions." She later recorded violin and vocals for the track "DIA" from Billy Corgan's album *The Future Embrace*, and created the costumes for his music video for the track "Walking Shade". In retrospect, Autumn felt working with both artists and promoting their albums had "stunted" her musical career, and she disliked the drug use that she had witnessed on Love's tour. In September 2004, her father died from lung cancer, even though he had quit smoking twenty years earlier. Near the end of 2004, she was filmed for an appearance on an episode of HGTV's *Crafters Coast to Coast*, showing viewers how to create faery wings and sushi-styled soap—both products she sold in her online "web design and couture fashion house", WillowTech House. Later in 2005, she recorded vocals and violin for "The Gates of Eternity" from Attrition's 2008 album *All Mine Enemys Whispers: The Story of Mary Ann Cotton*, a concept album focusing on the Victorian serial killer Mary Ann Cotton. Autumn later protested the release of the song, claiming that it was unfinished, "altered without her permission," and had been intended only as a possible collaboration with Martin Bowes.

2006–09: *Opheliac, Laced/Unlaced,* and *A Bit O' This & That*

The title of *Opheliac* is a reference to Shakespeare's character Ophelia (above) from the play *Hamlet*, whom Autumn felt a connection to, and the archetype of the "self-destructive" woman.

Autumn released the limited-edition EP *Opheliac*, a demo to her concept album of the same name, through her own label, Traitor Records; while the *Opheliac* EPs were being shipped, Autumn claimed that her offices had been robbed, causing the delay in the album release and the shipping of the EPs. In January 2006, she performed a song from the album, "Misery Loves Company", on the Chicago-based television station WGN, before the album's release by the German label Trisol Music Group on October 23 of the same year. She recorded *Opheliac* because "it was the documentation of a completely life-changing and life-ending experience". At one time, Autumn did have plans to film a music video for her song "Liar", which included "bloody bathtubs". Her favorite song on *Opheliac* is "The Art of Suicide" because she felt it was "the most honest" and "most complete thing [she has] written." Her song "Opheliac" appeared on the 2007 albums *13th Street: The Sound of Mystery, Vol. 3*, published by ZYX Music, and *Fuck the Mainstream, Vol. 1*, published by Alfa Matrix on June 19.

She released several more EPs and albums. November 2006 saw the release of the EP *Liar/Dead Is the New Alive*, which featured remixes of songs from *Opheliac* and new material. Her March 2007 album, *Laced/Unlaced*, consisted of two discs: *Laced*, the re-release of *On a Day...*, and *Unlaced*, new songs for the electric violin. She decided to re-release *On a Day* as *Laced* because she "felt that it made a nice contrast to the metal shredding fiddle album, "Unlaced," and [...] loved that it was the perfect representation of "then" versus "now." Five months later, she released *A Bit O' This & That*: a compilation album of her covers, including songs from The Beatles and The Smiths, classical pieces, and her own songs. In 2008, she released the EP *4 o'Clock*, which contained remixes of songs from *Opheliac*, new songs, and a reading from her autobiographical novel *The Asylum for Wayward Victorian Girls*. She also released another EP, *Girls Just Wanna Have Fun & Bohemian Rhapsody*, the same year. A year later, Autumn broke away from Trisol Music Group to join The End Records and re-release *Opheliac* in the United States on October 27, 2009; previously, it was only available there as an import. The re-release included extras such as pictures, bonus tracks, an excerpt from *The Asylum for Wayward Victorian Girls*, and a video.

In addition to releasing her own material, Autumn collaborated with other musicians. She appeared on the Adult Swim cartoon *Metalocalypse* as a guest artist in 2006 and on the subsequent 2007 album *The Dethalbum*. She contributed backing vocals and violin to the track "Dry" by Die Warzau and made an appearance in the band's music video for "Born Again". She played violin on the song "UR A WMN NOW" from OTEP's 2009 album, *Smash the Control Machine*. Additionally, two of her tracks appeared in film soundtracks: "Organ Grinder" from *4 o'Clock* on the European edition of *Saw III* and a remixed version of "Dead Is The New Alive" from *Opheliac* on the international version of *Saw IV*.

2010–present: *Fight Like A Girl*

In June 2010, Autumn released the acronym of her upcoming album, *F.L.A.G.*, on Twitter, before revealing the full title as *Fight Like A Girl*. She explained the concept behind "fighting like a girl" as self-defense without honor or rules. Planned to be "a bit more violent... bloodier [and]...a little more metal," *Fight Like A Girl* acts as a continuation of *Opheliac* and has the inmates fighting back against their abusers. On August 30, 2010, she announced that she would be undergoing jaw surgery and expected to have recovered by November. Which she did and concluded her North American Tour following her recovery.

Influences and musical style

Autumn in Frankfurt, 2007

A classically trained musician, Autumn draws influence from plays, novels, and history, particularly the Victorian era. She enjoys the works of Shakespeare, Elizabeth Barrett Browning and her husband Robert, and Edgar Allan Poe. She incorporates sounds resembling Victorian machinery such as locomotives, which she noted was "sort of a steampunk thing". While a young Autumn cited Itzhak Perlman as an influence because of the happiness she believed he felt when he played, her main musical influence and inspiration is the English violinist Nigel Kennedy. Her favorite singer is Morrissey from The Smiths. She takes inspiration for her songs from her life experiences and mixes in "layers and layers of references, connections, other stories and metaphors".

Autumn describes her music and style as "Psychotic Vaudeville Burlesque." She alternatively labels her music and style as "Victoriandustrial", a term she coined, and glam rock because of her use of glitter onstage. According to Autumn, her music "wasn't meant to be cutesy" and is labeled as industrial mainly because of her use of drums and yelling. Labeled as steampunk, neo-Victorian, and Industrial Gothic, her music encompasses a wide range of styles. The 2002 album *Enchant* drew on "new age chamber music, trip-hop baroque, and experimental space pop" while the 2006 release *Opheliac* featured "cabaret, electronic, symphonic, new age, and good ol' rock & roll (and heavy on the theatrical bombast)." Her vocal range registers from contralto to dramatic soprano.

For her live performances, which she calls dinner theatre because of her practice of throwing tea and tea-time snacks offstage, Autumn makes use of burlesque—"a show that was mainly using humour and sexuality to make a mockery of things that were going on socially and politically"—to counterbalance the morbid topics such as abuse and self-mutilation. She incorporates handmade costumes, fire tricks, theatrics, and a female backing band, The Bloody Crumpets: Veronica Varlow, Captain Maggot, The Blessed Contessa, Aprella, and formerly Little Lucina and the model Ulorin Vex. Her wish for the live shows is to be an "anti-repression statement" and empowerment.

Public image

While naturally a blonde, Autumn dyed her hair purple at seventeen, before progressing to orange, red, and then pink.

Autumn has bipolar disorder, which caused her to experience drastic mood swings, insomnia, and auditory hallucinations, and takes medication for it. Some of her songs—"Manic Depression", "Swallow", and "Misery Loves Company" from *Opheliac*—deal with living with the disorder. While she would "prefer to not have it [...] and probably be a lot happier," she believes that it gives her a different perspective on life and plans to "use it for all it's worth so that [she is] not a victim of it." Autumn experienced abuse, which began when she was six years old, and is a survivor of rape. She keeps a ritual of drawing a heart on her cheek as a symbol of protection and reminder of her humanity.

Autumn identifies as asexual. She went vegetarian at age eleven after being unable to rationalize why she should eat farm animals but not her pet; in her late-teens, she turned vegan. She believes that there is a link between the treatment of women and animals in society. She cares for two pet rats, Sir Edward and Basil, and a cat named Fish/Fishy, and endorses companies such as Manic Panic and Samson Tech.

Hospitalization and autobiographical novel

Returning from Courtney Love's 2004 tour, Autumn resumed working on her own career and became pregnant, although she had been on birth control. Terrified of pregnancy and childbirth and unwilling to pass on her bipolar disorder, she decided to have an abortion. Later, she attempted suicide, which caused her to be admitted to a psychiatric ward at a Los Angeles hospital and kept on suicide watch. On her experience there, she commented: "No one tried to break me out or contact me, and I wasn't allowed to call anyone. Now, I watch *One Flew Over the Cuckoo's Nest*, and realise it's actually a pretty accurate portrayal of a modern-day asylum."

After being released, she had her cell block number tattooed on her arm as a way of remembering what happened to her and penned her autobiographical novel, *The Asylum for Wayward Victorian Girls*, which was published in 2010. Because of the book's nature as an autobiography, its release was delayed because some did not want it published. Based on her diary written in red crayon while institutionalized, the book incorporated talking rats and the diary of a fictional Victorian inmate named "Emily". Autumn explained that "one of the main messages is" that many of the patients were not insane and that the subject of mental illness remains misunderstood.

Discography

Albums

- *On a Day...* (1997, re-released in *Laced/Unlaced* in 2007)
- *Enchant* (2003, re-released 2007)
- *Your Sugar Sits Untouched* (2005, CD and poetry book)
- *Opheliac* (2006, re-released 2009)
- *Laced/Unlaced* (2007)
- *A Bit o' This & That* (2007)
- *Fight Like a Girl* (TBA)

EPs and singles

- *Chambermaid* (2001)
- *By the Sword* (2001)
- *Opheliac EP* (2006, preview EP)
- *Liar/Dead Is the New Alive* (2006)
- *4 o'Clock* (2008)
- *Girls Just Wanna Have Fun & Bohemian Rhapsody* (2008)

Guest contributions

- Backing vocals and violin on the album *America's Sweetheart* (2003) by Courtney Love
- Backing vocals and violin on the album *The Future Embrace* (2004) by Billy Corgan
- Violin on the album *The Dethalbum* (2007) by Dethklok
- Song "Organ Grinder" on the European edition of the *Saw III* soundtrack
- Remix version of "Dead Is The New Alive" on the international version

of the *Saw IV* soundtrack
- Violin on the track "UR A WMN NOW" on OTEP's fourth album, *Smash the Control Machine* (2009)
- Vocals and violin on the song "Dry" by Die Warzau

Source (edited): "http://en.wikipedia.org/wiki/Emilie_Autumn"

J. M. Barrie

Sir James Matthew Barrie, 1st Baronet, OM (9 May 1860 – 19 June 1937) was a Scottish author and dramatist, best remembered today as the creator of Peter Pan. The child of a family of small-town weavers, he was educated in Scotland. He moved to London, where he developed a career as a novelist and playwright. There he met the Llewelyn Davies boys who inspired him in writing about a baby boy who has magical adventures in Kensington Gardens (included in *The Little White Bird*), then to write *Peter Pan, or The Boy Who Wouldn't Grow Up*, a "fairy play" about this ageless boy and an ordinary girl named Wendy who have adventures in the fantasy setting of Neverland. This play quickly overshadowed his previous work and although he continued to write successfully, it became his best-known work, credited with popularising the name *Wendy*, which was very uncommon previously. Barrie unofficially adopted the Davies boys following the deaths of their parents. Before his death, he gave the rights to the Peter Pan works to Great Ormond Street Hospital, which continues to benefit from them.

Childhood and adolescence

Barrie was born in Kirriemuir, Angus, to a conservative Calvinist family. His father David Barrie was a modestly successful weaver. His mother, Margaret Ogilvy, had assumed her deceased mother's household responsibilities at the age of eight. Barrie was the ninth child of ten (two of whom died before he was born), all of whom were schooled in at least the three Rs, in preparation for possible professional careers. He was a small child (he only grew to 5 ft 3½ in. according to his 1934 passport), and drew attention to himself with storytelling.

When he was 6 years old, Barrie's next-older brother David (his mother's favourite) died two days before his 14th birthday in an ice-skating accident. This left his mother devastated, and Barrie tried to fill David's place in his mother's attentions, even wearing David's clothes and whistling in the manner that he did. One time Barrie entered her room, and heard her say 'Is that you?' 'I thought it was the dead boy she was speaking to,' wrote Barrie in his biographical account of his mother, *Margaret Ogilvy* (1896), 'and I said in a little lonely voice, "No, it's no' him, it's just me."' Barrie's mother found comfort in the fact that her dead son would remain a boy forever, never to grow up and leave her. Despite evidence to the contrary, it has been speculated that this trauma induced psychogenic dwarfism, and was responsible for his short stature and apparently asexual adulthood. Eventually Barrie and his mother entertained each other with stories of her brief childhood and books such as *Robinson Crusoe*, works by fellow Scotsman Walter Scott, and *The Pilgrim's Progress*.

At the age of 8, Barrie was sent to The Glasgow Academy, in the care of his eldest siblings Alexander and Mary Ann, who taught at the school. When he was 10 he returned home and continued his education at the Forfar Academy. At 13, he left home for Dumfries Academy, again under the watch of Alexander and Mary Ann. He became a voracious reader, and was fond of penny dreadfuls, and the works of Robert Michael Ballantyne and James Fenimore Cooper. At Dumfries he and his friends spent time in the garden of Moat Brae house, playing pirates 'in a sort of Odyssey that was long afterwards to become the play of *Peter Pan*'. They formed a drama club, producing his first play *Bandelero the Bandit*, which provoked a minor controversy following a scathing moral denunciation from a clergyman on the school's governing board.

Literary career

Peter Pan statue in Kensington Gardens, London

Barrie wished to pursue a career as an author, but was dissuaded by his family — who wished him to have a profession such as the ministry, telling him it's what David would have done, had he been alive. With wise advice from Alec, he was able to work out a compromise. He was to attend a university, but would study literature. He enrolled at the University of Edinburgh, where he wrote drama reviews for Edinburgh Evening Courant. He was extremely introverted, and was shy about the fact he was in college and only approximately five feet. He would go on to graduate with his M.A. on April 21, 1882.

He worked for a year and a half as a staff journalist in Nottingham following a job advertisement found by his sister in *The Scotsman*, then returned to Kirriemuir, using his mother's stories about the town (which he called 'Thrums') for a piece submitted to the newspaper *St. James's Gazette* in London. The editor 'liked that Scotch thing', so Barrie wrote a series of them, which served as the basis for his first novels: *Auld Licht Idylls* (1888), *A Window in Thrums* (1890), and *The Little Minister* (1891). The stories depicted the "Auld Lichts", a strict religious sect that his grandfather had once belonged to. Literary criticism of these early works has been unfavourable, tending to disparage them as sentimental and nostalgic depictions of a parochial Scotland far from the realities of the industrialised nineteenth century, but they were popular enough to establish Barrie as a very successful writer. After the success of the "Auld Lichts", he printed *Better Dead* (1888) privately and at his own expense, and it failed to sell. His two 'Tommy' novels, *Sentimental Tommy* (1896) and *Tommy and Grizel* (1900), were about a boy and young man who clings to childish fantasy, with an unhappy ending.

Meanwhile, Barrie's attention turned increasingly to works for the theatre, beginning with a biography of Richard Savage and written by both Barrie and H.B. Marriott Watson (performed only once, and critically panned). He immediately followed this with *Ibsen's Ghost* (or *Toole Up-to-Date*) (1891), a parody of Henrik Ibsen's dramas *Hedda Gabler* and *Ghosts* (unlicensed in the UK until 1914, it had created a sensation at the time from a single 'club' performance). The production of Barrie's play at Toole's Theatre in London was seen by William Archer, the translator of Ibsen's works into English, who enjoyed the humour of the play and recommended it to others. His third play, *Walker, London* (1892), helped him be introduced to a young actress named Mary Ansell. Although he was unsure about his own suitability for marriage, he proposed to her and they were married on July 9, 1894. He got Ansell a Saint Bernard puppy, who would play a part in the novel *The Little White Bird* (or *Adventures in Kensington Gardens*). He also gave Ansell's Christian name to many characters in novels.

Barrie also authored *Jane Annie*, a failed comic opera for Richard D'Oyly Carte (1893), which he begged his friend Arthur Conan Doyle to revise and finish for him. In 1901 and 1902 he had back-to-back successes: *Quality Street*, about a responsible 'old maid' who poses as her own flirtatious niece to win the attention of a former suitor returned from the war; and *The Admirable Crichton*, a critically acclaimed social commentary with elaborate staging, about an aristocratic household shipwrecked on a desert island, in which the butler naturally rises to leadership over his lord and ladies for the duration of their time away from civilization.

The first appearance of Peter Pan came in *The Little White Bird*, which was serialised in the United States, then published in a single volume in the UK in 1901. Barrie's most famous and enduring work, *Peter Pan, or The Boy Who Wouldn't Grow Up*, had its first stage performance on 27 December 1904. This play introduced audiences to the name *Wendy*, which was inspired by a young girl, Margaret Henley, who called Barrie 'Friendy', but could not pronounce her *R*s very well and so it came out as 'Fwendy'. It has been performed innumerable times since then, was developed by Barrie into the 1911 novel *Peter and Wendy*, and has been adapted by others into feature films, musicals, and more. The Bloomsbury scenes show the societal constraints of late Victorian middle-class domestic reality, contrasted with Neverland, a world where morality is ambivalent. George Bernard Shaw's description of the play as 'ostensibly a holiday entertainment for children but really a play for grown-up people', suggests deeper social allegories at work in *Peter Pan*.

In April 1929 Barrie specified that the copyright of the Peter Pan works should go to the nation's leading children's hospital, Great Ormond Street Hospital in London. The current status of the copyright is somewhat complex.

Barrie had a long string of successes on the stage after *Peter Pan*, many of which discuss social concerns. *The Twelve Pound Look* shows a wife divorcing a peer and gaining an independent income. Other plays, such as *Mary Rose* and a subplot in *Dear Brutus* revisit the image of the ageless child. Later plays included *What Every Woman Knows* (1908). His final play was *The Boy David* (1936), which dramatised the Biblical story of King Saul and the young David. Like the role of Peter Pan, that of David was played by a woman, Elisabeth Bergner, for whom Barrie wrote the play.

Barrie used his considerable income to help finance the production of commercially unsuccessful stage productions. Along with a number of other playwrights, he was involved in the 1909 and 1911 attempts to challenge the censorship of the theatre by the Lord Chamberlain.

Acquaintances

Barrie travelled in high literary circles, and in addition to his professional collaborators, he had many famous friends. Novelist George Meredith was an early social patron. He had a long correspondence with fellow Scot Robert Louis Stevenson, who lived in Samoa at the time, but the two never met in person. George Bernard Shaw was for several years his neighbour, and once participated in a Western that Barrie scripted and filmed. H. G. Wells was a friend of many years, and tried to intervene when Barrie's marriage fell apart. Barrie met Thomas Hardy through Hugh Clifford while he was staying in London.

After the First World War Barrie sometimes stayed at Stanway House. He paid for the pavilion at Stanway cricket ground. Barrie founded an amateur cricket team for his friends. Arthur Conan Doyle, Wells, and other luminaries such as Jerome K. Jerome, G. K. Chesterton, A. A. Milne, Walter Raleigh, A. E. W. Mason, E. V. Lucas, Maurice Hewlett, E. W. Hornung, P. G. Wodehouse, Owen Seaman, Bernard Partridge, Augustine Birrell, Paul du Chaillu, and the son of Alfred Tennyson played in the team at various times. The team was called the Allahakbarries, under the mistaken belief that 'Allah akbar' meant 'Heaven help us' in Arabic (rather than 'God is great').

Barrie befriended Africa explorer Joseph Thomson and Antarctica explorer Robert Falcon Scott. He was godfather to Scott's son Peter, and was one of the seven people to whom Scott wrote letters in the final hours of his life following his successful – but doomed – expedition to the South Pole. Barrie was so proud of the letter that he carried it around for the rest of his life. In the note, Barrie was instructed to take care of Scott's wife, Kathleen, and son, Peter.

In 1896, his agent, Addison Bright persuaded him to meet with Broadway producer Charles Frohman. Frohman would become not only his financial backer, but a close friend as well. Frohman, who was responsible for producing the debut of *Peter Pan* in both England and the U.S., as well as other productions of Barrie's plays, famously declined a lifeboat seat when the *RMS Lusitania* was sunk by a German U-boat in the North Atlantic. Actress Rita Jolivet, who stood with Frohman, George Vernon and Captain Alick Scott at the end, recalled Frohman quoting his greatest hit, *Peter Pan*: "Why fear death? It is the most beautiful adventure that life gives us." On a common impulse, they all moved closer together and joined hands just before a great wave swept them all off the deck. Jolivet alone survived.

Barrie met and told stories to the young daughters of the Duke of York, who would become Queen Elizabeth II and Princess Margaret.

Marriage

Barrie became acquainted with actress Mary Ansell in 1891 when he asked his friend Jerome K. Jerome for a pretty actress to play a role in his play *Walker, London*. The two became friends, and she joined his family in caring for him when he fell very ill in 1893 and 1894. They married in Kirriemuir on 9 July 1894, shortly after Barrie recovered, and Mary retired from the stage; but the relationship was reportedly unconsummated and the couple had no children. The marriage was a small ceremony in his parents' home, in the Scottish tradition. In 1900 Mary found Black Lake Cottage, at Farnham, Surrey, which became the couple's 'bolt hole' where Barrie could entertain his cricketing friends and the Llewelyn Daviesies. Beginning in mid 1908, Mary had an affair with Gilbert Cannan (an associate of Barrie's in his anti-censorship activities), including a visit together to Black Lake Cottage, known only to the house staff. When Barrie learned of the affair in July 1909, he demanded that she end it, but she refused. To avoid the scandal of divorce, he offered a legal separation if she would agree not to see Cannan any more, but she still refused. Barrie sued for divorce on the grounds of infidelity, which was granted in October 1909. A few of Barrie's friends, knowing how painful the divorce was for him, wanted to avoid bad press. They wrote to newspaper editors asking them not to publish the story (only three papers did).

Llewelyn Davies family

The Arthur Llewelyn Davies family played an important part in Barrie's literary and personal life. It consisted of the parents Arthur (1863–1907) and Sylvia (1866–1910) (daughter of George du Maurier), and their five sons: George (1893–1915), John (Jack) (1894–1959), Peter (1897–1960), Michael (1900–1921), and Nicholas (Nico) (1903–1980).

Barrie became acquainted with the family in 1897, meeting George and Jack (and baby Peter) with their nurse (nanny) Mary Hodgson in London's Kensington Gardens. He lived nearby and often walked his Saint Bernard dog Porthos in the park. He entertained the boys regularly with his ability to wiggle his ears and eyebrows, and with his stories. He did not meet Sylvia until a chance encounter at a dinner party in December. She told Barrie that Peter had been named after the title character in her father's play, *Peter Ibbetson*. He became a regular visitor at the Davies household and a common companion to the woman and her boys, despite the fact that he and she were each married. In 1901, he invited the Davies family to Black Lake Cottage, where he produced an album of captioned photographs of the boys acting out a pirate adventure, entitled *The Boy Castaways of Black Lake Island*. Barrie had two copies made, one of which he gave to Arthur, who misplaced it on a train. The only surviving copy is held at the Beinecke Rare Book and Manuscript Library at Yale University.

Peter Pan was invented only to entertain George and Jack. Since Peter was a baby, Barrie would say, amusing himself and the kids, that Peter could fly. Barrie told them babies were birds before they were born; parents put bars on nursery windows to keep the little ones from flying away. This grew into a tale of a baby who did fly away, not realizing that he was no longer a bird. From this, Peter Pan was born.

Arthur Llewelyn Davies died in 1907, and 'Uncle Jim' became even more involved with the Daviesies, providing financial support to them. (His income from *Peter Pan* and other works was easily adequate to provide for their living expenses and education.) Following Sylvia's death in 1910, Barrie claimed that they had been engaged to be married. Her will indicated nothing to that effect, but specified her wish for 'J. M. B.' to be trustee and guardian to the boys, along with her mother Emma, her brother Guy Du Maurier, and Arthur's brother Compton. It expressed her confidence in Barrie as the boys' caretaker and her wish for 'the boys to treat him (& their uncles) with absolute confidence & straightforwardness & to talk to him about everything.' When copying the will informally for Sylvia's family a few months later, Barrie inserted himself elsewhere: Sylvia had written that she would like Mary Hodgson, the boys' nurse, to continue taking care of them, and for 'Jenny' (referring to Hodgson's sister) to come and help her; Barrie instead wrote 'Jimmy' (Sylvia's nickname for him). Barrie and Hodgson did not get along well, but they served as surrogate parents until the boys went to university and Jack was married.

Barrie also had friendships with other children, both before he met the Davies boys and after they had grown up, and there has since been speculation that Barrie was a paedophile. However, there is no evidence of any such conduct, nor that he was suspected of it at the time. A reason for the suspicion of pedophilia is because of the novel *The Little White Bird*, in which in one scene Captain W. helps David undress for bed. Nico, the youngest of the brothers, flatly denied that Barrie ever behaved inappropriately. 'I don't believe that Uncle Jim ever experienced what one might call "a stirring in the undergrowth" for anyone — man, woman, or child,' he stated. 'He was an innocent — which is why he could write Peter Pan.' His relationships with the surviving Davies boys continued well beyond their childhood and adolescence.

The statue of Peter Pan in Kensington Gardens, erected in secret overnight for May Morning in 1912, was supposed to be modelled upon old photographs of Michael dressed as the character. However, the sculptor Sir George Frampton decided to use a different child as a model, leaving Barrie disappointed with the result. 'It doesn't show the devil in Peter,' he said.

Barrie suffered bereavements with the boys, losing the two to whom he was closest in their early twenties. George was killed in action (1915) in World War I. Michael, with whom Barrie corresponded daily while at boarding school and university, drowned (1921) with his friend and possible lover, Rupert Buxton, at a known danger spot at Sandford Lock near Oxford, one month short of his 21st birthday. Some years after Barrie's death, Peter compiled his *Morgue* from family letters and papers, interpolated with his own informed comments in his family and their relationship with Barrie.

Death

Barrie died of pneumonia on 19 June 1937 and is buried at Kirriemuir next to his parents and two of his siblings. He left the bulk of his estate (excluding the Peter Pan works, which he had previously given to Great Ormond Street Hospital) to his secretary Cynthia Asquith. His birthplace at 4 Brechin Road is maintained as a museum by the National Trust for Scotland.

Source (edited): "http://en.wikipedia.org/wiki/J._M._Barrie"

Janeane Garofalo

Janeane Garofalo (pronounced /dʒəˈniːn gəˈrɒfəloʊ/; born September 28, 1964) is an American stand-up comedian, actress, political activist and writer. She is the former co-host on the now defunct Air America Radio's *The Majority Report*. Garofalo continues to circulate regularly within New York City's local comedy and performance art scene.

Early life

Garofalo was born in Newton, New Jersey, the daughter of Joan and Carmine Garofalo. Her mother was a secretary, in the petrochemical industry, who died of cancer when Janeane was 24. Her father is a former executive at Exxon. Garofalo was raised as a conservative Catholic and is of Italian and Irish descent. She grew up in various places, including Ontario, California; Madison, New Jersey, where she graduated from Madison High School; and Katy, Texas. Garofalo is quoted as having disliked life in Houston because of the heat and humidity and the emphasis on prettiness and sports in high school.

While studying history at Providence College, Garofalo entered a comedy talent search sponsored by the Showtime cable network, winning the title of "Funniest Person in Rhode Island." Her original gimmick was to read off her hand, which was not successful in subsequent performances. Dreaming of earning a slot on the writing staff of the TV show *Late Night With David Letterman*, she became a professional standup upon graduating from college with degrees in History and American Studies. She struggled for a number of years, even working briefly as a bike messenger in Boston.

Garofalo has described herself thus: "I guess I just prefer to see the dark side of things. The glass is always half empty. And cracked. And I just cut my lip on it. And chipped a tooth."

Entertainment career

Stand-up comedy

Garofalo officially began her career in stand-up comedy in the late 1980s during the pre-grunge era. Her appearance was often in line with late 1980s style: disheveled with thick black glasses and unkempt hair. Her comedy is often self-deprecating; she has made fun of popular culture and the pressures on women to conform to body image ideals promoted by the media.

Garofalo's comedy shows involve her and her notebook, which is filled with years' worth of article clippings and random observations she references for direct quotes during her act. Garofalo has said that she does not tell jokes as much as make observations designed to get laughs. She was part of the alternative comedy scene in Los Angeles in the early 1990s, appearing at Un-Cabaret and other venues and co-created the Eating It comedy series which ran at Luna Lounge on the Lower East Side of New York City between 1995 and 2005. She did a one-hour stand-up special, "If You Will," at Seattle's Moore Theatre, that aired on *Epix* in June 2010 and was released on DVD in September 2010.

During her filmed stand-up show in Seattle, she brought up her ten-year asexual relationship with her boyfriend, describing herself as having no interest in sex whatsoever.

Television

Garofalo's big break came in 1990 after meeting Ben Stiller at Canter's Deli in Los Angeles, where they were hanging out with stand-up friends. They bonded over their "love of SCTV, early Saturday Night Live and Albert Brooks."

Her television series debut was on the short-lived *Ben Stiller Show* on Fox in 1992, on which she was a cast member alongside longtime friends Bob Odenkirk, Andy Dick, and David Cross. A chance meeting on the set of that show led her to be offered the role of Paula on *The Larry Sanders Show* on HBO, earning her two Emmy Award nominations in 1996 and 1997.

After *The Ben Stiller Show* was cancelled, Garofalo joined the cast of *Saturday Night Live (SNL)* for its 1994–95 season. She left *SNL* in March 1995 (mid-season) after only six months, saying that the experience left her "anxious and depressed" and that a sexist attitude pervaded the show and she called many of the sketches "juvenile and homophobic.". According to *New York Magazine*, Garofalo was "largely stuck in dull, secondary wife and girlfriend roles" and her friends said that she considered the stint "the most miserable experience of [her] life."

Following *SNL*, Garofalo appeared in a plethora of guest star roles: the grown-up daughter of the Buchmans on the final episode of *Mad About You*; Jerry Seinfeld's female counterpart (and, briefly, fiancée) Jeannie Steinman on *Seinfeld*; a correspondent on Michael Moore's *TV Nation* and a former girlfriend of Dave Foley's character on *Newsradio*. Two television pilots starring Garofalo, the 2003 ABC show *Slice O'Life* about a reporter consigned to sappy human interest stories appearing at the end of news broadcasts, and the 2005 NBC program *All In*, based on the life of poker star Annie Duke, were not picked up by their respective networks.

Throughout the 2005–2006 television season, Garofalo appeared on *The West Wing* as Louise Thornton, a controversial campaign adviser to the fictional Democratic presidential nominee. Garofalo participated in the series' first live episode, most of which was a debate televised live on the East Coast and then reshot live for the West. Garofalo's character can be seen walking backstage advising before the start of each debate. In 2006, she provided the voice for the animated character "Bearded Clam" on Comedy Central's *Freak Show*. In 2007, she wrote a dedication for the mini-book included in the six-DVD box-set of the 1994 cult series *My So-Called Life*.

In 2009, Garofalo joined the cast of *24*, where she starred as Janis Gold.

Garofalo was a cast member of the *Criminal Minds* short-lived spinoff TV series *Criminal Minds: Suspect Behavior*.

In 2010, Garofalo joined the cast of Ideal as Tilly.

Films

Garofalo's breakthrough into film came in 1994's *Reality Bites* as Winona Ryder's Gap-managing best friend Vickie. The role helped solidify Garofalo's status as a Generation X icon. In 1996, Garofalo earned a starring role in the critically acclaimed *The Truth About Cats & Dogs*, a variation on *Cyrano de Bergerac* which featured Uma Thurman in the lead role as a beautiful but dimwitted model, while Garofalo played a highly intelligent radio host. Initially an independent film, it became a studio movie when Thurman was signed. The film was a modest hit, but Garofalo disparages it to this day, saying:

> I think it's soft and corny, and the soundtrack makes you want to puke, and everybody's dressed in Banana Republic clothing. The original script and the original intent was very different than what it wound up being when it became a studio commercial film. It was originally supposed to be a small-budget independent film where there would be much more complexity to all the characters, and Abby and the guy don't wind up together at the end.

Based on the success of this film, director Cameron Crowe then offered her the leading lady role in *Jerry Maguire* with Tom Cruise if she could lose weight; after trimming down, however, she learned that Renée Zellweger had won the part instead. Garofalo turned down the role of Gale Weathers in Wes Craven's *Scream* because she thought the film would be too violent: "I said I didn't want to be in a movie where a teen girl was disemboweled. I didn't know it turned out so good, and it was a funny movie." Garofalo had also been David Fincher's first choice for the role of Marla Singer in the film *Fight Club*, but she turned it down, uncomfortable with the film's sexual content.

Before *The Truth About Cats & Dogs*, she was visible from television work and supporting roles in films such as *Reality Bites*, *Bye Bye Love* and *Now and Then*, and a leading role in *I Shot a Man in Vegas*. Garofalo has had a variety of leading, supporting and cameo roles in *Cop Land*, *Wet Hot American Summer*, *Romy and Michele's High School Reunion*, *Dogma*, *The Cable Guy*, *Half-Baked*, *Mystery Men*, *The Wild*, and *Clay Pigeons*.

Garofalo played the leading role in the *The MatchMaker*, a 1997 film about the misadventures of a cynical American woman who reluctantly visits Ireland. In 2002, she played Catherine Connolly in *The Laramie Project*. A puppet version of Garofalo appeared (and was graphically killed off) in the movie *Team America: World Police*; while Garofalo was irritated by the parody, she was more upset by the filmmaker's lack of correspondence. "I ran into them in the street, Trey and the other guy, and I said to them, 'The least you could do is send me a puppet.' And they said OK, took my address down ... and never sent me a puppet! So while Team America bothered me, the fact they didn't send me my puppet, that bothered me even more."

Garofalo had a segment in several episodes of the 2007 season of *The Henry Rollins Show*. These took place in her apartment, much in the same way Rollins' take place at his house. In 2007, she provided the voice of Colette, a chef in the Pixar/Disney feature film *Ratatouille*. Garofalo affected a pronounced French accent in the role, highlighted by her character's soliloquy about being the only female chef in the all-male kitchen.

She made cameo appearances in *The Guitar* in 2008 and *Labor Pains* in 2009.

Political views

Garofalo has been open and outspoken regarding her progressive political views. In an interview for *Geek Monthly* magazine, she stated that she grew up conservative in a conservative family.

She has appeared with political figures such as Ralph Nader (whom she supported in the 2000 election, but opposed in 2004) and Jello Biafra at various events. Garofalo now describes herself as an atheist, and has participated in a radio interview by Freethought Radio, a show by the Freedom From Religion Foundation.

She became more prominent as an activist when she voiced opposition to what became the 2003 Iraq War, appearing on CNN and Fox News to discuss it. She said that she was approached by groups such as MoveOn.org and Win Without War to go on TV, because these organizations say that the networks were not allowing antiwar voices to be heard. Garofalo and the other celebrities who appeared at the time said they thought their fame could lend attention to that side of the debate. Her appearances on cable news prior to the war garnered her praise from the left and spots on the cover of *Ms.* and *Venus Zine*. Garofalo has had frequent on-air political disputes with Bill O'Reilly, Brian Kilmeade, and Jonah Goldberg.

Prior to the 2003 Iraq War, she took a position on the threat posed by Saddam Hussein. For example, in an interview with Tony Snow on a February 23, 2003 episode of *Fox News Sunday*, Garofalo said of the Iraqi dictator:

" Yes, I think lots of people are eager to obtain weapons of mass destruction. But there's no evidence that he (Hussein) has weapons of mass destruction. There's been no evidence of him testing nuclear weapons. We have people that are in our face with nuclear weapons. We've got " Iran and North Korea. We've got a problem with Pakistan. You know, I don't know what to say about that. There's a whole lot of people that are going nuclear. And I think that Saddam Hussein is actually, with the evidence, the least able to use nuclear weapons and the least obvious offender in that area at this moment.

In March 2003, she took part in the Code Pink anti-war march in Washington, D.C. That fall, she served as emcee at several stops on the *Tell Us the Truth* tour, a political-themed concert series featuring Steve Earle, Billy Bragg, Tom Morello, and others. Throughout the year, Garofalo also actively campaigned for Howard Dean.

While on Fox News' program *The Pulse*, O'Reilly asked Garofalo what she would do if her predictions that the Iraq war would be a disaster were to turn out wrong. Garofalo stated:

" I would be so willing to say I'm sorry, I hope to God that I can be made a buffoon of, that people will say you were wrong, you were a fatalist, and I will go to the White House on my knees on cut glass and say, hey, you were right, I shouldn't have doubted you. "

In April 2009, Garofalo drew criticism when she denounced the Tea Party protests, saying:

" Let's be very honest about what this is about. This is not about bashing Democrats. It's not about taxes. They have no idea what the Boston Tea Party was about. They don't know their history at all. It's about hating a black man in the White House. That is racism straight up. This is nothing but a bunch of teabagging rednecks. "

In response to the controversy Garofalo has continued to criticize Tea Party protesters, and has been reported to open her shows with "If there's any tea baggers here, welcome, and as always, white power."

Air America Radio

In late March 2004, Garofalo became a co-host for Air America Radio's new show *The Majority Report* alongside Sam Seder. The early days of Air America Radio are chronicled in the documentary *Left of the Dial*, which includes a debate between Garofalo and her conservative father Carmine, who was initially a regular guest on *The Majority Report*.

Garofalo was criticized by Rick Ross and some of her listeners for comments she made on her April 28, 2006 show, supporting the Scientology-linked New York Rescue Workers Detoxification Project, a controversial treatment for workers suffering ailments from 9/11 clean-up efforts in New York City. Garofalo cited her reason for leaving the show as precipitated by such "unrecoverable" on-air arguments with Seder. She also said that she regards Seder as a better radio broadcaster than she, and therefore a better choice to continue *The Majority Report*.

Her last broadcast as co-host of *The Majority Report* aired on July 21, 2006. Since then, she has made a few appearances on *The Sam Seder Show*. She called on October 4, 2006, to discuss the Mark Foley scandal and on October 31, 2006, she was in studio, where she portrayed Katherine Harris in a Halloween skit. Garofalo has continued to portray Harris on the show in numerous appearances following the 2006 elections.

Garofalo made a series of appearances in New York and Los Angeles with Henry Rollins and Air America personality Marc Maron in April 2007.

Filmography

Movies

- *Late for Dinner* (1991)
- *That's What Women Want* (1992)
- *Reality Bites* (1994)
- *Bye Bye Love* (1995)
- *I Shot a Man in Vegas* (1995)
- *Coldblooded* (1995)
- *Now and Then* (1995)

- *Sweethearts* (1996)
- *The Truth About Cats & Dogs* (1996) (Abbey Barnes)
- *The Cable Guy* (1996)
- *Larger Than Life* (1996)
- *Touch* (1997)
- *Romy and Michele's High School Reunion* (1997) (Heather Mooney)
- *The MatchMaker* (1997) (Marcy Tizard)
- *Cop Land* (1997)
- *Clay Pigeons* (1998)
- *Kiki's Delivery Service* (1998) (voice - English version)
- *Thick as Thieves* (1998)
- *Permanent Midnight* (1998)
- *Half Baked* (1998)
- *The Thin Pink Line* (1998)
- *The Bumblebee Flies Anyway* (1999)
- *Torrance Rises* (1999)
- *Can't Stop Dancing* (1999)
- *Mystery Men* (1999) (The Bowler)
- *Dogma* (1999)
- *The Independent* (1999)
- *200 Cigarettes* (1999)
- *The Minus Man* (1999)
- *Dog Park* (2000)
- *Steal This Movie!* (2000) (Anita Hoffman)
- *Titan A.E.* (2000) (voice)
- *The Adventures of Rocky and Bullwinkle* (2000)
- *What Planet Are You From?* (2000)
- *The Laramie Project* (2001)
- *The Search for John Gissing* (2001)
- *Wet Hot American Summer* (2001) (Beth)
- *Martin & Orloff* (2002)
- *Big Trouble* (2002) (Officer Monica Romero)
- *Manhood* (Showtime; 2003)
- *Wonderland* (2003)
- *Nobody Knows Anything!* (2003)
- *Jiminy Glick in Lalawood* (2004)
- *Duane Hopwood* (2005)
- *Nadine in Date Land*, Oxygen Network; (2005) (Nadine Barnes)
- *Stay* (2005) (Dr. Beth Levy)
- *The Wild* (2006) (voice)
- *Ratatouille* (2007) (voice)
- *Southland Tales* (2007)
- *The Ten* (2007)
- *Girl's Best Friend* (2008)
- *Labor Pains (Made For TV Film)* (2009)

Short films
- *Suspicious* (1994)
- "Angel Mine" (1996 music video)
- *The Cherry Picker* (2000)
- *Housekeeping* (2001)
- *Junebug and Hurricane* (2004)

Documentaries
- *New York: A Documentary Film* (1999)
- *Outlaw Comic: The Censoring of Bill Hicks* (2003)
- *Dangerous Living: Coming Out In The Developing World* (2003)
- *Gigantic (A Tale of Two Johns)* (2003)
- *Left of the Dial* (2005), HBO
- *I Am Comic* (2010)

Television
- *The Tom Green Show*
- *The Henry Rollins Show*
- *Outlaw Comic: The Censoring of Bill Hicks* (2003)
- *TV Nation*, NBC, Fox
- *The Chris Rock Show*, HBO
- *The Larry Sanders Show*, HBO (Paula)
- *The Ben Stiller Show*, Fox
- *Tales of the City*, BBC/PBS (Coppola Woman)
- *Small Doses*, Comedy Central
- *Saturday Night Live*, NBC
- *Seinfeld*, NBC
- *The Simpsons* (Herself)
- *Newsradio*, NBC
- *Space Ghost Coast to Coast*, Cartoon Network
- *Law & Order*, NBC
- *Late Night with Conan O'Brien*
- *Now with Bill Moyers*, PBS
- *The Daily Show*
- *Janeane Garofalo*, HBO (1997) (hour-long standup special)
- *Behind the Scenes at Daria*, MTV (2000)
- *Late Show with David Letterman* (Guest Host)
- *The Late Late Show with Craig Ferguson*
- *The King of Queens*, CBS (Trish)
- *Shorties Watching Shorties*, Comedy Central
- *The Tonight Show with Jay Leno*, NBC
- *Primetime Glick*, Comedy Central
- *Mad About You* (series finale) (Mabel)
- *Home Improvement*
- *The Belzer Connection*, SciFi Channel
- *The Minnesota Half-Hour Smile Hour*
- *Pilot Season*
- *Tanner on Tanner*, Sundance Channel (Herself)
- *Stella*, Comedy Central
- *Felicity*
- *Hannity & Colmes*, Fox News
- *Real Time with Bill Maher*, HBO
- *Comic Remix*
- *Jimmy Kimmel Live*, ABC
- *The Rosie O'Donnell Show*
- *Dennis Miller Live*
- *The Sopranos*, HBO (Herself)
- *King of the Hill*, Fox
- *Ellen*, ABC
- *Dinner for Five*, IFC
- *Mr. Show with Bob and David: Fantastic Newness*, HBO (1996)
- *The West Wing*, NBC (2005) (Louise Thornton)
- *In the Life*, PBS (2005)
- *Strangers with Candy* (Cassie Pines)
- *The Adventures of Pete and Pete*, Nickelodeon
- *Two and a Half Men*, CBS
- *Tom Goes To The Mayor* (2006)
- *Rove* (2007 & 2009)
- *24* (2009)
- *Head Case*, Starz (2009)
- *Greek* (2009)
- *Spicks and Specks*
- *Never Mind the Buzzcocks* (Series 23 Episode 1), BBC 2 (2009)
- *John Oliver's New York Stand Up Show* (2010)
- *Stella* (Episode 8)
- *Ideal* (Series 6), BBC Three (2010) (Tilly)
- *Criminal Minds: Suspect Behavior* (Series regular, 2011) (SSA Beth Griffith)

Source (edited): "http://en.wikipedia.org/wiki/Janeane_Garofalo"

Keri Hulme

Keri Hulme (born March 9, 1947) is a New Zealand writer, best known for *The Bone People*, her only novel.

Early life

Hulme was born in Christchurch, in New Zealand's South Island. The daughter of a carpenter and a credit manager, she was the eldest of six children. Her parents were of English, Scottish, and Māori (Ngāi Tahu) descent. "Our family comes from diverse people: Kai Tahu, Kāti Mamoe (South Island Maori iwi); Orkney islanders; Lancashire folk; Faroese and/or Norwegian migrants," Hulme told *Contemporary Women Poets* Her early education was at North New Brighton Primary School and Aranui High School. Her father died when she was 11 years old.

Hulme worked as a tobacco picker in Motueka after leaving school. She began studying for an honours law degree at the University of Canterbury in 1967, but left after four terms and returned to tobacco picking.

Career

By 1972, she decided to begin writing full-time, but, despite family support, was forced to go back to work nine months later. She continued writing, some of her work appearing under the pseudonym Kai Tainui. During this time, she continued working on her novel, *The Bone People*, ultimately published in February 1984. The novel was returned by several publishers before being accepted by the Spiral Collective. It won the 1984 New Zealand Book Award for Fiction and the Booker Prize in 1985.

Hulme was a writer-in-residence at the University of Otago in 1978, and at the University of Canterbury in 1985. She lives in Okarito, on New Zealand's West Coast. Hulme has been the Patron of the Republican Movement of Aotearoa New Zealand since 1996. She identifies as an aromantic asexual and is an atheist.

Awards

- *Katherine Mansfield Memorial Award*, 1975;
- *New Zealand Literary Fund grant*, 1975, 1977, 1979;
- *Maori Trust Fund Prize*, 1978
- *East-West Centre Award*, 1979;
- *Book of the Year Award'*, 1984
- *Mobil Pegasus Prize*, 1985
- *Booker Prize*, 1985
- *Scholarship in Letters*, 1990;

Works

Novels

- *The Bone People* (1984)
- *Bait* and *On the Shadow Side* (in progress; referred to by Hulme as 'twinned novels')

Poetry

- *The Silences Between (Moeraki Conversations)* (1982)
- *Lost Possessions* (1985)
- *Strands* (1992)

Short Stories

- *Te Kaihau: The Windeater* (1986)
- *Te Whenua, Te Iwi/The Land and The People* (1987)
- *Homeplaces: Three Coasts of the South Island of New Zealand* (1989)
- *Stonefish* (2004)

Source (edited): "http://en.wikipedia.org/wiki/Keri_Hulme"

Morrissey

Steven Patrick Morrissey (born 22 May 1959), known as **Morrissey**, is an English singer and lyricist. He rose to prominence in the 1980s as the lyricist and vocalist of the alternative rock band The Smiths. The band was highly successful in the United Kingdom but broke up in 1987, and Morrissey began a solo career, making the top ten of the UK Singles Chart on ten occasions. Widely regarded as an important innovator in indie music, Morrissey has been described by music magazine *NME* as "one of the most influential artists ever," and *The Independent* has stated "most pop stars have to be dead before they reach the iconic status he has reached in his lifetime." Pitchfork Media has called him "one of the most singular figures in Western popular culture from the last twenty years."

Morrissey's lyrics have been described as "dramatic, bleak, funny vignettes about doomed relationships, lonely nightclubs, the burden of the past and the prison of the home." He is also noted for his unique baritone vocal style (though he is known to sometimes use falsetto for emphasis), his quiff haircut and his dynamic live performances. His forthright, often contrarian opinions, especially on the subject of race, have led to a number of media controversies, and he has also attracted media attention for his advocacy of vegetarianism and animal rights.

Biography

Early life: 1959–76

Morrissey was born on 22 May 1959 at Park Hospital in Davyhulme, Urmston, Lancashire to Irish Catholic immigrants who had emigrated to England with his only sibling, elder sister Jackie, a year prior to his birth. His father, Peter Morrissey, was a hospital porter and his mother, Elizabeth Dwyer, was an assistant librarian. Morrissey was predominantly raised within inner-city Manchester; his family first lived at Harper Street in Hulme before moving to Queen's Square, near Moss Side, in 1965. In 1969, when many of the old streets and tenements were facing demolition, Morrissey's parents moved to a three-bedroomed house on King's Road in the suburb of Stretford.

As a child, Morrissey developed a number of interests and role models that distinguished him from his peers, including female singers and pop stars like Dusty Springfield, Sandie Shaw, Marianne Faithfull and Billy Fury. He was also interested in the "kitchen sink"-style social realism of late 1950s and early 1960s television plays, *Coronation Street's* Elsie Tanner, actor James Dean, along with authors Oscar Wilde and Shelagh Delaney. The Moors Murders—which involved a young working-class couple, Ian Brady and Myra Hindley, who had abducted, raped and killed three children and two teenagers from the Manchester area between July 1963 and October 1965—devastated and scandalised the city when the matter came to trial in April–May 1966, and this collective trauma is said to have made a profound and lasting impression on Morrissey growing up.

In adolescence, Morrissey has said his athletic ability saved him to a large degree from bullying. Still, he has described this period as a time when he was often lonely and depressed. As a teenager, he began taking prescription drugs to help combat the depression that would later follow him throughout his life. He attended St. Mary's Secondary Modern School and Stretford Technical School, where he passed three O levels, including English Literature. He then worked briefly for the Inland Revenue, but ultimately decided to "go on the dole."

Of his youth, Morrissey said, "Pop music was all I ever had, and it was completely entwined with the image of the pop star. I remember feeling the person singing was actually with me and understood me and my predicament." From 1974, he frequently wrote letters to music magazines like *Melody Maker* and the *NME*, giving his forthright opinions on various bands. Morrissey would sometimes venture out to see bands at local Manchester venues; the first such occasion being T. Rex at Belle Vue in 1972. He was taken there by his father, fearing for his safety in the notoriously rough district. Morrissey has described the occasion as "messianic and complete chaos."

Early bands and published books:

1977–81

Throughout the 1970s, a teenage Morrissey acted as president of the UK branch of the New York Dolls fan club. He articulated his love for the group in the documentary *New York Doll*: "Some bands grab you and they never let you go and, no matter what they do, they can never let you down... the Dolls were that for me." This New York Dolls influence made Morrissey an early convert to punk rock. Morrissey, then still with forename, briefly fronted The Nosebleeds in 1978, who by that time included Billy Duffy on guitar (Duffy went on to form the post-punk band The Cult). They played a number of concerts, including one supporting Magazine, which resulted in an *NME* review by Paul Morley. Morrissey also founded The Cramps fan club, the Legion of the Cramped, with another enthusiast for their music, Lindsay Hutton, but he progressively scaled down his involvement in the club over time because of the increasing amount of time he was devoting to his own musical career.

Morrissey wrote several songs with Duffy, such as "Peppermint Heaven," "I Get Nervous" and "(I Think) I'm Ready for the Electric Chair," but none were recorded during the band's short lifespan, which ended the same year. After The Nosebleeds' split, Morrissey followed Duffy to join Slaughter & the Dogs, briefly replacing original singer Wayne Barrett. He recorded four songs with the band and they auditioned for a record deal in London. After the audition fell through, Slaughter & the Dogs became Studio Sweethearts without Morrissey.

The singer interrupted his music career at around this time, focusing instead on writing on popular culture. He published two works with Babylon Books: *The New York Dolls* (1981), about his favourite band; and *James Dean is Not Dead* (1983), about actor James Dean's brief career. A third book, *Exit Smiling*, which was actually written first (in 1980) and which dealt with obscure B movie actors, was initially rejected and remained unpublished until 1998.

The Smiths: 1982–87

In early 1982, Morrissey met the guitarist Johnny Marr and the two began a songwriting partnership: "We got on absolutely famously. We were very similar in drive." After recording several demo tapes with future Fall drummer Simon Wolstencroft, in autumn 1982 they recruited drummer Mike Joyce. They also added bass player Dale Hibbert, who provided the group with demo recording facilities at the studio where he worked as a factotum. However, after two gigs Marr's friend Andy Rourke replaced Hibbert on bass because neither Hibbert's bass playing nor his personality "meshed" with the rest of the group. Signing to independent record label Rough Trade Records, they released their first single, "Hand in Glove", in May 1983. It was championed by DJ John Peel, as were all their later singles, but it failed to chart. The follow-up singles "This Charming Man" and "What Difference Does It Make?" fared better when they reached numbers 25 and 12 respectively on the UK Singles Chart. Aided by praise from the music press and a series of studio sessions for Peel and David Jensen at BBC Radio 1, The Smiths began to acquire a dedicated fan base. In February 1984, they released their debut album *The Smiths,* which reached number two on the UK Albums Chart.

In 1984, the band released two non-album singles: "Heaven Knows I'm Miserable Now" (their first UK top-ten hit) and "William, It Was Really Nothing". The year ended with the compilation album *Hatful of Hollow*. This collected singles, B-sides and the versions of songs that had been recorded throughout the previous year for the Peel and Jensen shows. Early in 1985 the band released their second album, *Meat is Murder*, which was their only studio album to top the UK charts. The single-only release "Shakespeare's Sister" reached number 26 on the UK Singles Chart, though the only single taken from the album, "That Joke Isn't Funny Anymore", was less successful, barely making the top 50.

During 1985, the band undertook lengthy tours of the UK and the US while recording the next studio record, *The Queen is Dead*. The album was released in June 1986, shortly after the single "Bigmouth Strikes Again". The record reached number two in the UK charts. However, all was not well within the group. A legal dispute with Rough Trade had delayed the album by almost seven months (it had been completed in November 1985), and Marr was beginning to feel the stress of the band's exhausting touring and recording schedule. Meanwhile, Rourke was fired in early 1986 for his use of heroin. Rourke was temporarily replaced on bass guitar by Craig Gannon, but he was reinstated after only a fortnight. Gannon stayed in the band, switching to rhythm guitar. This five-piece recorded the singles "Panic" and "Ask" (with Kirsty MacColl on backing vocals) which reached numbers 11 and 14 respectively on the UK Singles Chart, and toured the UK. After the tour ended in October 1986, Gannon left the band. The group had become frustrated with Rough Trade and sought a record deal with a major label, ultimately signing with EMI, which drew criticism from the band's fanbase.

In early 1987, the single "Shoplifters of the World Unite" was released and reached number 12 on the UK Singles Chart. It was followed by a second compilation, *The World Won't Listen,* which reached number two in the charts – and the single "Sheila Take a Bow," the band's second (and last during the band's lifetime) UK top-10 hit. Despite their continued success, personal differences within the band – including the increasingly strained relationship between Morrissey and Marr – saw them on the verge of splitting. In July 1987, Marr left the group and auditions to find a replacement proved fruitless.

By the time the group's fourth album *Strangeways, Here We Come* was released in September, the band had split up. The breakdown in the relationship has been primarily attributed to Morrissey's annoyance with Marr's work with other artists and to Marr's growing frustration with Morrissey's musical inflexibility. *Strangeways* peaked at number two in the UK, but was only a minor US hit, though it was more successful there than the band's previous albums.

Solo career: 1988–97

In March 1988, a mere six months after the Smiths' final album, Morrissey released his first solo album, *Viva Hate.* To create the album, Morrissey teamed up with former Smiths producer Stephen Street, Vini Reilly of Durutti Column (and formerly of the Nosebleeds), and drummer Andrew Paresi. *Viva Hate* reached number one upon release, supported by the singles "Suedehead" and "Everyday Is Like Sunday". *Viva Hate* was certified Gold by the RIAA on 16 November 1993.

Morrissey initially planned to release a follow-up album entitled *Bona Drag* after releasing a few holdover singles from the *Viva Hate* sessions. As such, he released "The Last of the Famous International Playboys," "Interesting Drug," and "Ouija Board, Ouija Board" over the course of 1989. The first two of these became top ten hits. However, by the end of 1989 it became apparent that he would not be able to put out an album of new material soon enough. Morrissey decided to scrap the idea of a full-length LP and release *Bona Drag* as a compilation of singles and B-sides instead. The album collected these early singles along with further non-album cuts such as "November Spawned a Monster," "Piccadilly Palare," "Disappointed" and the B-side "Hairdresser on Fire."

After a falling out with Stephen Street, Morrissey recruited the production aid of Clive Langer and songwriting services of Mark E. Nevin, of Fairground Attraction, for the studio follow-up to *Viva Hate,* entitled *Kill Uncle.* The album peaked at number eight on the UK charts. The two singles released in promotion of the album, "Our Frank" and "Sing Your Life," failed to break the Top 20 on the singles charts reaching number 26 and number 33 respectively. Morrissey released two non-album singles, "Pregnant for the Last Time" and "My Love Life." The band Morrissey assembled in 1991 for his *Kill Uncle* tour went on to record 1992's hit album *Your Arsenal.* Composition duties were split between guitarists Boz Boorer and Alain Whyte, who have been the core of Morrissey's band until the later stages of his comeback period. *Your Arsenal* was produced by former David Bowie guitarist Mick Ronson, and earned a Grammy Award nomination for Best Alternative Album. The album peaked at number four on the UK charts, with two of its three singles, "We Hate It When Our Friends Become Successful" and "You're the One for Me, Fatty," both debuting in the Top 20 in the UK.

By 1994, Morrissey had suffered the loss of three people close to him: Mick Ronson, Tim Broad and Nigel Thomas. Channelling his grief, Morrissey wrote and recorded his second number one album in the UK, *Vauxhall and I.* Years after the release, Morrissey acknowledged that he felt at the time that it was going to be his last album, and that not only was it the best album he'd ever made but that he would never be able to top it in the future. One of the album's songs, "The More You Ignore Me, the Closer I Get," reached number eight in the UK and number 46 in the US. That year, he also released a single "Interlude" in duet with Siouxsie Sioux of Siouxsie and the Banshees. Following the success of *Vauxhall and I* Morrissey began work on *Southpaw Grammar* in early 1995. When released in August, the album was a hit, reaching number four in the UK. However, both of its singles failed to chart in the Top 20. The nature of the album was different to past Morrissey releases. Musically, the inclusion of two tracks which surpass the ten minute mark, the near two and half minute drum solo courtesy of Spencer Cobrin which opens the track "The Operation" and the sampling of a Shostakovich symphony have led some to dub the album as 'Morrissey's flirtation with prog-rock.' Some critics were impressed by this apparent attempt at progression, while others dismissed the longer tracks as mere self-indulgence. With the exception of the single "Sunny" in that December it would be another year before Morrissey released a new album or single.

In 1996, Joyce took Morrissey and Marr to court, claiming that he had not received his fair share of recording and performance royalties. Morrissey and Marr had claimed 40% each of the Smiths' recording and performance royalties and allowed ten percent each to Joyce and Rourke. Composition royalties were not an issue, as Rourke and Joyce had never been credited as composers for the band. Morrissey and Marr claimed that the other two members of the band had always agreed to that split of the royalties as they had consented to an account of the royalties sent to Joyce during the band's existence, but initially the High Court and then the Court of Appeal found in favour of Joyce and ordered that he be paid over £1 million in back pay and receive twenty-five percent henceforth. As Smiths' royalties had been frozen for two years, Rourke settled for a smaller lump sum to pay off his debts and continued to receive ten percent. While the judge in the case described Morrissey as "devious, truculent and unreliable," he did not state that the singer had been dishonest. Morrissey claimed that he was "...under the scorching spotlight in the dock, being drilled..." with questions such as " 'How dare you be successful?' 'How dare you move on?'" He stated that "The Smiths were a beautiful thing and Johnny [Marr] left it, and Mike [Joyce] has destroyed it." Morrissey appealed against the verdict, but was not successful.

Morrissey returned on a new record label in 1997 with the single "Alma Matters" in promotion of his album *Maladjusted.* Though the single was hailed by some as a return to form for Morrissey, the resulting album is considered both a commercial and critical disappointment. The album peaked at number eight in the UK album charts and its further two singles, "Roy's Keen" and "Satan Rejected My Soul" both peaked outside the UK Top 30. Morrissey would not release another studio album for seven years.

Comeback: 2003–10

Despite the absence of any record deal, Morrissey undertook a world tour throughout 2002, with dates across the US, Europe, Australia, and Japan. Setlists consisted of material from his Smiths and solo years, and new songs that would later be recorded for his seventh studio album. It was during this time that Channel 4 filmed *The Importance of Being Morrissey,* a documentary which eventually aired in 2003. In June 2003, it was revealed Sanctuary Records had given Morrissey the one-time reggae label Attack Records to record new material and to sign new artists. *You Are the Quarry* was released in 2004. The album peaked at number two on the UK album chart and number 11 on the Billboard album chart in the United States. Guitarist Alain Whyte described the work as a mix between *Your Arsenal* and *Vauxhall and I,* and the album received strong reviews. The first single, "Irish Blood, English Heart," reached number three in its first week of sales in the UK singles chart. This was the highest placing chart position for Morrissey in his entire career at that point. Three other hit singles followed: "First of the Gang to Die," "Let Me Kiss You," and "I Have Forgiven Jesus." With the release of "I Have Forgiven Jesus," Morrissey along with McFly became the only artists to score four top-10 hits in the UK singles chart that year. The album has since sold over a million copies, making the album his most successful one, solo or with the Smiths. To coincide with the release of the album, Morrissey embarked on an accompanying tour spanning several continents from April to November. In August 2004, Morrissey was slated to headline a week-long set of shows on Craig Kilborn's *The Late Late Show.* Morrissey did not perform every night of the weeklong series due to a throat illness. He did, however, perform the following week. The performance at the Manchester Evening News Arena on Morrissey's 45th birthday was recorded and released on the DVD *Who Put the M in Manchester?* in 2005.

Morrissey's eighth studio album, *Ringleader of the Tormentors,* was recorded in Rome and released on 3 April 2006. Upon release, it debuted at number one in the UK album charts and number 27 in the US. The album yielded four hit singles: "You Have Killed Me," "The Youngest Was the Most Loved," "In the Future When All's Well," and "I Just Want to See the Boy Happy." Originally Morrissey was to record the album with producer Jeff Saltzman, however he could not undertake the project. Producer Tony Visconti, of T.Rex and David Bowie fame, took over the production role and Morrissey announced that the album was "the most beautiful—perhaps the most gentle, so far." *Billboard magazine* described the album as showcasing "a thicker, more rock-driven sound." Morrissey attributes this change in sound to new guitarist Jesse Tobias. The subsequent 2006 international tour included more than two dozen gigs in the UK, including concerts at the London Palladium. Morrissey was scheduled to appear at the 2005 Benicassim festival in Spain but pulled out at the last minute. In January 2007, the BBC confirmed that it was in talks with Morrissey for him to write a song for the 2007 Eurovision Song Contest. If an agreement could be made, Morrissey would be writing the song for someone else, rather than performing it himself, a BBC spokesperson claimed. The following month, the BBC ruled this out, and stated Morrissey would not be part of Britain's Eurovision entry.

In early 2007, Morrissey left Sanctuary Records and embarked on a *Greatest Hits* tour. The tour ran from 1 February 2007 to 29 July 2008 and spanned 106 concerts over 8 different countries. Morrissey cancelled 11 of these dates, including a planned six consecutive shows at the Roundhouse in London, due to "throat problems." The tour consisted of three legs, the first two encompassing the US and Mexico were supported by Kristeen Young from February to October while the remainder featured Girl in a Coma. The final leg was a small scale European tour that saw Morrissey headlining the O2 Wireless Festival in Hyde Park, London on 4 July and culminated in Morrissey playing at the Heatwave Festival in Tel Aviv, Israel on 29 July.

After a show in Houston, Texas, on the first leg of the tour Morrissey rented out the Sunrise Sound Studio to record "That's How People Grow Up." The song was recorded with producer Jerry Finn rather than previous producer Tony Visconti for a future single and inclusion on an upcoming album. In an interview on BBC Radio 5 Live with Visconti, the producer stated that his new project would be Morrissey's next album, though that this would not be forthcoming for at least a year. However, in an interview with the BBC News website in October 2007, Morrissey said that the album was already written and ready for a possible September 2008 release and confirmed that his deal with Sanctuary Records had come to an end. In December he signed a new deal with Decca Records, which included a *Greatest Hits* album and a newly-recorded album to follow in autumn 2008. Upon signing with Decca, Morrissey released "That's How People Grow Up" as the first single off of his new *Greatest Hits* album. Despite lukewarm reviews, especially in the *NME*, the lack of airplay on British radio (except on XFM), and even the incredulity of fan sites, "That's How People Grow Up" reached the Top 15, reaching number 14 on the British charts. Reviews for the Greatest Hits compilation were very mixed; reviewers noted that the album only includes songs which reached the Top 15 in the charts, putting the emphasis on new songs, making the CD more suitable for new listeners than for old fans. The album charted at number 5 in the British album chart on its week of release. A limited edition of the *Greatest Hits* album also featured an eight-track live CD which was recorded at the Hollywood Bowl in 2007. A second single from the *Greatest Hits*, "All You Need Is Me," was released in March. In May 2008, Morrissey parted ways with his manager of five years, Merck Mercuriadis, in favour of a new contract with IE Music, however by September Morrissey left the group and acquired the services of Irving Azoff.

Morrissey at SXSW, 2006.

On 30 May 2008, it was announced that Morrissey's ninth studio album, *Years of Refusal* would have 12 tracks and be produced by Jerry Finn. On 5 August 2008 it was reported that, although originally due in September, *Years of Refusal* had been postponed until February 2009, as a result of Finn's death and the lack of an American label to distribute the album.

On 15 August 2008, Warner Music Entertainment announced the upcoming release of *Morrissey: Live at the Hollywood Bowl,* a DVD documenting the live performance that took place at the historic Hollywood Bowl in Los Angeles, California, on 8 June 2007 on the first leg of Morrissey's 2007/2008 Greatest Hits tour. Morrissey greeted news of the DVD's release by imploring fans not to buy it. Originally due to be released 6 October 2008, the DVD has subsequently been delayed until 1 March 2009 by Warner Music according to HMV.

In November 2008, *Rolling Stone* magazine named Morrissey one of "The 100 Greatest Singers of All Time." The list was compiled from ballots cast by a panel of 179 "music experts," such as Bruce Springsteen, Alicia Keys and Bono, who were asked to name their 20 favourite vocalists. Morrissey was ranked 92.

In February 2009, following persistent rumours over preceding months of an imminent Smiths reunion, Morrissey was once again forced to deny that any such reunion would take place. In an interview with BBC Radio 2, he remarked that "people always ask me about reunions, and I can't imagine why... the past seems like a distant place, and I'm pleased about that." In a separate interview, with London radio station Xfm, Morrissey also stated that "chances were slim" that he himself would continue performing past the age of 55.

Years of Refusal was released worldwide on 16 February 2009 by the Universal Music Group. Upon release, it reached third place in the UK Albums Chart and 11 in the US Billboard 200. The record was widely acclaimed by critics, with comparisons made to *Your Arsenal* and *Vauxhall and I*. A review from Pitchfork Media noted that with *Years of Refusal,* Morrissey "has rediscovered himself, finding new potency in his familiar arsenal. Morrissey's rejuvenation is most obvious in the renewed strength of his vocals" and called it his "most venomous, score-settling album, and in a perverse way that makes it his most engaging." "I'm Throwing My Arms Around Paris" and "Something Is Squeezing My Skull" were released as the record's singles. The song "Black Cloud" features the guitar playing of Jeff Beck. Throughout 2009 Morrissey toured to promote the album. As part of the extensive Tour of Refusal, Morrissey followed a lengthy US tour with concerts booked in Ireland, Scotland, England, Russia. He had never before performed in Russia.

In April 2009, remastered editions of 1995's *Southpaw Grammar* and 1997's *Maladjusted* were released in the UK. These both featured a rearranged track listing with the inclusion of B-sides and outtakes, resulting in albums quite different to the original. They also featured new artwork and liner notes written by Morrissey. The reissues were available in the US from June that year.

October 2009 saw the release of a 2004–2009 B-Sides collection, named *Swords*. The album peaked at 55 on the UK albums chart, and Morrissey later called the compilation 'a meek disaster.' On the second date of the UK tour to promote *Swords,* Morrissey collapsed with breathing difficulties upon finishing the opening song of his set, "This Charming Man," at the Oasis Centre, Swindon. He was discharged from the hospital the following day.

Following the completion of the *Swords* tour it was announced that Morrissey had fulfilled his contractual obligation to Universal Records and was without a record company. Shortly after this announcement, it was also revealed he had split with Front Line Management.

In July 2010, it was announced that EMI will reissue the 1990 album *Bona Drag* on its Major Minor imprint, resurrected specifically for the release. The release features six additional previously unreleased tracks, and was released on 4 October, entering at number 67 in the UK charts. The 1988 single "Everyday Is Like Sunday" was also reissued to coincide with the release on both CD and 7" vinyl formats.

2011 and future

In February 2011, EMI announced a brand new compilation – *Very Best of Morrissey* – would be released in April that year. The press release stated both the tracklist and artwork were chosen by Morrissey himself, and the single "Glamorous Glue" would also be reissued the same week with two previously unreleased songs.

In March 2011, it was announced Morrissey was now under the management of Ron Laffitte and would be headlining the Hop Farm Festival in July that year. Shortly after this announcement, a UK tour was unveiled – mainly consisting of small venues in the North of Britain plus Glastonbury Festival – taking place in June 2011. In July and August he is also touring venues in Europe. Only two exclusive festival dates, namely Hultsfred Festival in Sweden and Lokerse Feesten in Belgium, are announced.

Morrissey has stated that he has completed a 660-page autobiography which he intends to offer to publishers.

On 14 June 2011, Janice Long premiered three new Morrissey songs in session on her BBC Radio 2 program. Those songs are titled: "Action Is My Middle Name", "The Kid's a Looker" and "People Are The Same Everywhere".

On 24 June 2011, Morrissey played on the pyramid stage at Glastonbury. While he was there he criticised the UK Prime Minister David Cameron for attempting to stop the ban on wild animals performing in circuses, calling him a 'silly twit'.

Image and politics

Music industry feuds

Morrissey has criticised singers like Madonna, Elton John and George Michael, generally claiming their lyrics are pointless and they are more interested in being celebrities than in their music. He has also had disagreements with The Cure's Robert Smith, who stated "If Morrissey says not to eat meat, then I'll eat meat; that's how much I hate Morrissey." Lol Tolhurst, another founding member of the Cure, has claimed he likes Morrissey's music; however, he also said Smith is "quite justified in his ire", alleging their feud was instigated by Morrissey:
"We had never met Morrissey or the Smiths at that point and Morrissey made a very uncalled for remark concerning Robert in the English press. I never understood why as we or Robert had done nothing to upset him that I could think of, but after that it kind of snowballed.... Especially as journalists love feuds!!"
Morrissey also once openly wished *Morrissey & Marr: The Severed Alliance* author Johnny Rogan "ends his days very soon in an M3 pile-up." Neil Tennant of the Pet Shop Boys co-wrote two songs inspired by Morrissey's public stereotyping as miserable and unlovable ("Getting Away with It" and "Miserablism").

In 1994, Morrissey was criticised by Manic Street Preachers' bassist and lyricist Nicky Wire, in regards to comments Morrissey had made about immigration and national identity in NME. Other targets of his disapproval have been Band Aid, rap and rave music, and teenage pop stars. He once stated he disapproved of reggae – a criticism he later retracted, stating he was being facetious and he grew up partly on the classic singles released by the British reggae label Trojan in the early to mid-1970s.

Attitude towards political leaders

Morrissey has always been politically outspoken, directing his criticism at figures ranging from Oliver Cromwell, the British Royal Family, former British Prime Ministers Margaret Thatcher and Tony Blair and former U.S. President George W. Bush. He has criticised both the two main political parties of the United Kingdom, the Labour Party and the Conservative Party.

In a 1984 interview, Morrissey spoke of the then-Prime Minister, Margaret Thatcher: "She is only one person. She can be destroyed. It is the only remedy for this country at the moment." Morrissey's first solo album, *Viva Hate*, included a track entitled "Margaret on the Guillotine", a tongue-in-cheek jab at Thatcher. British police responded by searching Morrissey's home and carrying out an official investigation, while Simon Reynolds, who had interviewed Morrissey for *Melody Maker*, was questioned about the tone in which Morrissey had made certain remarks about Thatcher.

At a Dublin concert in June 2004, Morrissey caused controversy by announcing the death of former US President, Ronald Reagan and stating that he would have preferred it if the then current President, George W. Bush, had died. In October 2004, Morrissey released a statement urging American voters to vote for Democratic Party candidate John Kerry for President, calling this vote a "logical and sane move". Morrissey opined that "Bush has single-handedly turned the United States into the most neurotic and terror-obsessed country on the planet."

In February 2006, Morrissey said he had been interviewed by the Federal Bureau of Investigation (FBI) and by British intelligence after having spoken out against the American and British governments. Morrissey said that "They were trying to determine if I was a threat to the government, it didn't take them long to realise that I am not." During a January 2008 concert Morrissey remarked "God Bless Barack Obama" and ranted against Hillary Clinton after a performance of "The World Is Full of Crashing Bores."

In December 2010, he publicly supported Johnny Marr, who had stated that he forbade British Prime Minister, David Cameron, from liking the Smiths. Morrissey added "I would like to, if I may, offer support to Johnny Marr who has spoken out to the media this week against David Cameron. David Cameron hunts and shoots and kills stags – apparently for pleasure. It was not for such people that either *Meat Is Murder* or *The Queen Is Dead* were recorded; in fact, they were made as a reaction against such violence". In his statement, he also lambasted the British Royal Family, noting their continued violence toward animals (in their pursuit of hunting and their use of bearskin to make the hats of the British guards) and their utter irrelevance in British life. He referred to Prince William and his then fiancée Kate Middleton as "so dull as people that it is actually impossible to discuss them".

Accusations of racism

Morrissey was accused of racism throughout part of the 1980s and much of the 1990s, primarily due to the ambiguous lyrics in songs such as "Bengali in Platforms," "Asian Rut" and "The National Front Disco," the latter containing the lyric "England for the English." These criticisms also stemmed from Johnny Rogan's biography of the singer which claimed that, in his late teens, the singer wrote "I don't hate Pakistanis, but I dislike them immensely." In 2006 Liz Hoggard from *The Independent* argued that "Morrissey didn't help his case with an uneasy flirtation with gangster imagery: he took up boxing and was accompanied everywhere by a skinhead, named Jake." She claimed that the "man who abhorred violence became strangely fascinated by it." Encyclopædia Britannica argues that Morrissey's 1990s albums, including *Your Arsenal* (1992), *Vauxhall and I* (1994), *Southpaw Grammar* (1995) and *Maladjusted* (1997) "testified to a growing homoerotic obsession with criminals, skinheads, and boxers, a change paralleled by a shift in the singer's image from wilting wallflower to would-be thug sporting sideburns and gold bracelets."

A trigger for much of the criticism was Morrissey's performance at the first Madness *Madstock!* reunion concert at Finsbury Park, London, in 1992, in which he appeared on stage draped in the Union Flag, often associated with nationalism and the British far-right. As a backdrop for this performance, he chose a photograph of two female skinheads. The British music magazine *NME* responded to this performance with a lengthy examination of Morrissey's attitudes to race, claiming that the singer had "left himself in a position where accusations that he's toying with far-right/fascist imagery, and even of racism itself, can no longer just be laughed off with a knowing quip."

In the early days of the Smiths, Morrissey stated that "all reggae is vile," leading to the first reports of his alleged racism. He later explained that this was a tongue-in-cheek answer to "wind up the right-on 1980s NME" and that he grew up partly on the classic singles released by the British reggae label Trojan in the early to mid-1970s. The Smiths' "Panic," released in July 1986, fades out with the refrain "hang the DJ, hang the DJ, hang the DJ..." Rogan's biography reports that initial critical response to this content was interpreted as distaste for the increasing influence of rap and R&B over popular music at the time.

Morrissey has strongly rejected claims that he is racist, saying "If I am racist then the Pope is female. Which he isn't," and "If the National Front were to hate anyone, it would be me. I would be top of the list." He qualified that by saying that far-right rage "is simply their anger at being ignored in what is supposed to be a democratic society." In the 2002 documentary, *The Importance of Being Morrissey*, he posits the question, "Why on earth would I be racist? What would I be trying to achieve?" In the film, he also takes issue with those who fail to discern the subtlety of his supposedly racist lyrics, stating that "Not everybody is absolutely stupid."

In 1999, Morrissey commented on the rise of Austrian far-right politician Jörg Haider, stating "This is sad. Sometimes I don't believe we live in an intelligent world." In 2004 he signed the Unite Against Fascism statement, and in 2008 he made a personal donation of £75,000 to the organisers of the Love Music Hate Racism concert in Victoria Park, London, after the withdrawal of the *NME's* sponsorship left the event facing a financial shortfall.

In 2007, Morrissey sparked controversy by claiming British identity has disappeared because the country has been "flooded" by immigrants in his interview with *NME*. Morrissey's lawyers are now pressing legal action against *NME* for defamation, with the magazine declining to print a retraction or apology. Within days of issuing the writ against NME, Morrissey also released a detailed explanation of his side of the story via an online fanzine. The statement included a firmly worded rebuttal against the accusations of racism, a condemnation of racism itself and an exposition on his belief that NME's editor had deliberately staged and scandalised the outcome of the interview in an orchestrated attempt to boost the paper's "dwindling circulation." In 2008, Word Magazine was forced to apologise in court for an article by David Quantick that accused Morrissey of being a racist and a hypocrite.

In September 2010, during an interview with Simon Armitage in the Guardian's weekend magazine Morrissey described the treatment of animals in China as "absolutely horrific" and in reference to other reports of animal welfare violations in China he said, "you can't help but feel the Chinese are a subspecies." A spokesman for Love Music Hate Racism, which received a donation of £28,000 from the singer in 2008 after his apparently anti-immigration comments made in music magazine NME, said it would be unable to accept support from Morrissey again if he did not rescind or dispute the comments, saying: "It really is just crude racism. When you start using language like 'sub-species', you are entering into dark and murky water. I don't think we would, or could, ask him to come back after that."

Despite accusations of racism in the United Kingdom Morrissey maintains a large Latino fan base in the United States and in Los Angeles particularly. His height in popularity among U.S. Hispanics was the subject of William E Jones' documentary *Is It Really So Strange?* Morrissey himself has written about Mexico in his song of the same title and has stated his affection for the Mexican people in interviews.

Animal rights activism

Morrissey has been vegetarian since he was 11 years old. He has explained his vegetarianism by saying "If you love animals, obviously it doesn't make sense to hurt them." Morrissey is an advocate for animal rights and a supporter of People for the Ethical Treatment of Animals (PETA). In recognition of his support, PETA honoured him with the Linda McCartney Memorial Award at their 25th Anniversary Gala on 10 September 2005.

In January 2006, Morrissey attracted criticism when he stated that he accepts the motives behind the militant tactics of the Animal Rights Militia, saying "I understand why fur-farmers and so-called laboratory scientists are repaid with violence—it is because they deal in violence themselves and it's the only language they understand."

Morrissey has criticised people who are involved in the promotion of eating meat, specifically Jamie Oliver and Clarissa Dickson Wright – the latter already targeted by some animal rights activists for her stance on fox hunting. In response, Dickson-Wright stated "Morrissey is encouraging people to commit acts of violence and I am constantly aware that something might very well happen to me." The Conservative MP David Davis criticised these comments, saying that "any incitement to violence is obviously wrong in a civilised society and should be investigated by the police." On 27 March 2006, Morrissey released a statement that he would not include any concert dates in Canada on his world tour that year—and that he supported a boycott of all Canadian goods—in protest against the country's annual seal hunt, which he described as a "barbaric and cruel slaughter".

In 2009 he abandoned a stage at the Coachella Festival in California because of the smell of cooking meat. He later returned to finish his set.

In September 2010 he ignited a public controversy for describing Chinese people as a "subspecies" because of their treatment of animals. In an interview with British poet, playwright and novelist Simon Armitage he said: "Did you see the thing on the news about their treatment of animals and animal welfare? Absolutely horrific. You can't help but feel that the Chinese are a subspecies." He later made a statement saying "if anyone has seen the horrific and unwatchable footage of the Chinese cat and dog trade – animals skinned alive – then they could not possibly argue in favour of China as a caring nation. There are no animal protection laws in China and this results in the worst animal abuse and cruelty on the planet. It is indefensible."

Sexuality

Morrissey's sexuality has been a matter of conjecture, and this has been fuelled by many conflicting statements from the singer, none of which has ever explicitly stated his sexual orientation. *Encyclopædia Britannica* argues that he created a "compellingly conflicted persona (loudly proclaimed celibacy offset by coy hints of closeted homosexuality)" which has "made him a peculiar heartthrob." "Morrissey has always taken great pains to maintain the 'undecidable' nature of his sexuality." In 1983 he claimed to be "a kind of prophet for the fourth sex," on the grounds that he was "bored with men and ...bored with women." In 1984, he stated that he refused "to recognise the terms hetero-, bi-, and homo-sexual" because "everybody has exactly the same sexual needs." A 1984 Smiths article in *Rolling Stone* stated that Morrissey "admits he's gay," but Morrissey replied that it was news to him and the article used the term "fourth-gender" in its title.

The speculation was further fuelled by the frequent references to gay subculture and slang in his lyrics. In 2006, Liz Hoggard from *The Independent* noted, "Only 15 years after homosexuality had been decriminalised, his lyrics flirted with every kind of gay subculture"; for example, she claims that "This Charming Man" "is about age-gap, gay sex." Reviewer Stephen Thomas Erlewine claims lyrics to the Smiths single "Hand in Glove" contain very thinly "veiled references to homosexuality."

Throughout much of his career, he maintained in interviews that he was asexual and celibate. Johnny Marr stated in a 1984 interview that "Morrissey doesn't participate in sex at the moment and hasn't done so for a while, he's had a lot of girlfriends in the past and quite a few men friends." In 1986, Morrissey claimed that he was "dramatically, supernaturally, non-sexual." In a 1994 interview, he claimed that "sex is actually never in my life," and as such, he argued that "I have no sexuality." In 1995, he claimed "I'd like to have a sex life, if possible." In a 1997 interview, he revealed he had been in a relationship with someone for two years but that it had ended and the person in question had just stopped loving him. He did not reveal the sex of his partner or whether it was a sexual relationship. However, he did admit to caring deeply and he stated he had hoped he or she had shared similar feelings. In a 2006 *NME* interview, he stated he was no longer celibate, but he did not give any additional details. A 2006 article in UK paper *The Independent* stated the singer "...has even hinted at a late-blooming sex life." John Murphy of musicOMH has even speculated that the lyrics "Nothing entered me, 'til you came with the key" to Morrissey's 2006 song "You Have Killed Me" give reference to a sexual encounter he had.

Morrissey frequently tells interviewers who ask him about his sexuality the question is irrelevant to his music, or he gives an evasive or ambiguous response. While the debate over Morrissey's sexuality has become widespread on fan websites, including attempts to analyse the meaning of his ambiguous song lyrics, their attempts are often stymied because, as *The Times* critic Tom Gatti puts it, "Morrissey's music offers infinite capacity for interpretation" because "they are too flexible, too rich, too textured."

Legacy and influence
Morrissey is routinely referred to as an influential artist, both in his solo career and with the Smiths. The BBC has referred to him as "one of the most influential figures in the history of British pop," and the *NME* named the Smiths the "most influential artist ever" in a 2002 poll, even topping the Beatles. *Rolling Stone*, naming him one of the greatest singers of all time in a recent poll, noted that his "rejection of convention" in his vocal style and lyrics is the reason "why he redefined the sound of British rock for the past quarter-century." Morrissey's enduring influence has been ascribed to his wit, the "infinite capacity for interpretation" in his lyrics, and his appeal to the "constant navel gazing, reflection, solipsism" of generations of "disenfranchised youth," offering unusually intimate "companionship" to broad demographics. Journalist Mark Simpson calls Morrissey "one of the greatest pop lyricists – and probably *the* greatest-ever lyricist of desire – that has ever moaned" and observes that "he is fully present in his songs as few other artists are, in a way that fans of most other performers...wouldn't tolerate for a moment. Simpson also argues that "After Morrissey there could be no more pop stars. His was an impossible act to follow...[his] unrivalled knowledge of the pop canon, his unequaled imagination of what it might mean to be a pop star, and his breathtakingly perverse ambition to turn it into great art, could only exhaust the form forever." In 2006, he was voted the second greatest living British icon in a poll held by the BBC's *Culture Show*. The *All Music Guide to Rock* asserts that Morrissey's "lyrical preoccupations," particularly themes dealing with English identity, proved extremely influential on subsequent artists. Journalist Phillip Collins also described him as a major influence on modern music and "the best British lyricist in living memory."

Cultural historian Julian Stringer notes that the Smiths and Morrissey were a product of and a reaction against Thatcherism, and that their rise to fame "can be seen as the only sustained response that white, English pop/rock music was able to make against the Conservative Government's appropriation of white, English national identity; and that being the case, it is not really surprising that the response is utterly riddled with contradiction". Other scholars have responded favourably to Morrissey's work, including academic symposia at various universities including University of Limerick and Manchester Metropolitan University. Gavin Hopps, a research fellow and literary scholar at the University of St. Andrews, wrote a full-length academic study of Morrissey's work, calling him comparable to Oscar Wilde, John Betjeman, and Philip Larkin, and noting similarities between Morrissey and Samuel Beckett. The *British Food Journal* featured an article in 2008 that applied Morrissey's lyrics to building positive business relationships. A major book of academic essays edited by Eoin Devereux, Aileen Dillane and Martin Power, *Morrissey: Fandom, Representations and Identities*, which focuses on Morrissey's solo career, was published in 2011.

A *Los Angeles Times* critic wrote that Morrissey "patented the template for modern indie rock" and that many bands playing at the Coachella Valley Music and Arts Festival "would not be there – or at least, would not sound the same – were it not for him." Similarly, the critic Steven Wells called Morrissey "the man who more or less invented indie" and an artist "who more than anybody else personifies" indie culture. Stephen Thomas Erlewine of Allmusic writes that the Smiths and Morrissey "inspired every band of note" in the Britpop era, including Suede, Blur, Oasis, and Pulp. Other major artists including Jeff Buckley and Radiohead have also been influenced by Morrissey. Colin Meloy of the Decemberists, who recorded a 2005 EP of Morrissey covers titled *Colin Meloy Sings Morrissey,* acknowledged Morrissey's influence on his songwriting: "You could either bask in that glow of fatalistic narcissism, or you could think it was funny. I always thought that was an interesting dynamic in his songwriting, and I can only aspire to have that kind of dynamic in my songs." Brandon Flowers of the American Rock band The Killers has revealed his admiration for Morrissey on several different occasions and admits that his interest for writing songs about murder such as "Jenny Was A Friend of Mine" and "Midnight Show" traces back to Morrissey singing about loving 'the romance of crime' in the song Sister I'm A Poet. Flowers quoted "I studied that line a lot. And it's kind of embedded in me."

In addition to the numerous pop culture homages to Smiths songs, bands The Ordinary Boys and The Boy Least Likely To chose their names based on solo Morrissey songs.
Source (edited): "http://en.wikipedia.org/wiki/Morrissey"

Paula Poundstone

Paula Poundstone (born December 29, 1959) is an American stand-up comedienne.

Early life
Poundstone was born in Huntsville, Alabama, and her family moved to Sudbury, Massachusetts. Poundstone attended Lincoln-Sudbury Regional High School, but dropped out to pursue a show business career. Her jobs have included busing tables and working as a bicycle messenger.

Career
She started doing stand-up comedy on open-mic nights in Boston in 1979, eventually relocating to California. She

usually performs dressed in a suit and tie. In 1984, Poundstone was cast in the movie *Hyperspace* but she did not follow through on a potential acting career. Instead she became better known as a comedian and began appearing on several talk shows. In 1989, she won the American Comedy Award for "Best Female Stand-Up Comic." In 1990, she wrote and starred in an HBO special called *Cats, Cops and Stuff*, for which she won a CableACE Award. She worked as a political correspondent for the *Tonight Show* during the 1992 US Presidential campaign and did the same for *The Rosie O'Donnell Show* in 1996.

In 1993, Poundstone won a second CableACE Award, began writing a regular column, "Hey, Paula!" for *Mother Jones* (1993–1998), and had a variety show, *The Paula Poundstone Show*, on ABC (which lasted only two episodes). She was also a regular panelist for the game shows *Hollywood Squares* and *To Tell the Truth*.

She has also done some voiceover work, voicing Judge Stone on *Science Court* (also known as *Squigglevision*), an edutainment cartoon series done in the Squigglevision style and aired on Saturday mornings on ABC Kids in 1997. Staying with Tom Snyder Productions (makers of Science Court) she was also made the voice of *Home Movies* mom character Paula Small for the show's first five episodes, which aired on UPN. Between the show's 1999 UPN cancellation and 2000 revival on Cartoon Network she chose to leave the show, being replaced by Janine Ditullio. The character's name and some of her appearance were modeled after Poundstone.

She is number 88 on Comedy Central's 2004 list of the 100 greatest stand-ups of all time, and number 7 on *Maxim* magazine's list of "Worst Comedians of All Time."

She had her own Bravo special as part of their three-part Funny Girls series, along with Caroline Rhea and Joan Rivers, titled "Look What the Cat Dragged In."

Around the same time as her Bravo special, Poundstone also released her first book, *There Is Nothing in this Book That I Meant to Say*. Described as an autobiography that is "part memoir, part monologue," the book intertwines historical biographies with anecdotes from her own life.

She has appeared frequently as a panelist on the radio news quiz show *Wait Wait... Don't Tell Me!* on National Public Radio. Also, she is a regular guest on *A Prairie Home Companion*, often appearing in shows in Los Angeles or at joke shows.

Poundstone released her first comedy CD, "I Heart Jokes," in 2009.

Personal life

Poundstone adopted her first child, Thomas, in 1993. In 1997, she adopted two girls, Toshia and Allison. Later, she adopted another son, to whom she refers as "Thomas E."

Poundstone was a foster mother to several other children until 2001, when she was barred from the foster care program following a conviction of child endangerment for driving under the influence with a child passenger. Since then she has used the incident—and the resulting publicity—as the source for some of her comedic material.

Poundstone labels herself asexual. She stated her asexuality in an interview with the *Dallas Voice* in June 2007, saying "I'm totally an asexual human being. I haven't dated anyone". In her memoirs she wrote,

I am not, at this time, a virgin myself, but I don't like sex, so I abstain, which should certainly be at least a cousin to virgin, perhaps deserving something in an honorary title. Should I become a beloved hero in my time, my followers could refer to me as "virginish." ...The idea that I'd get to my bed and there'd be someone in there with whom I was supposed to have an activity is horrifying to me. It's a safe bet that I'm not good at sex, that I do it wrong.

Poundstone frequently refers to cats in her comedy and on her website. She shares her home with numerous cats and supports Alley Cat Allies, a nonprofit advocacy organization dedicated to transforming communities to protect and improve the lives of cats.

On her website, Poundstone states that she is an atheist.

Arrest

In 2001, Poundstone was arrested on a felony warrant for three counts of committing a lewd act on an unidentified girl under age 14. The Los Angeles County District Attorney's office also stated that Poundstone was charged with endangering two other unidentified girls and two boys. Few details were released, but the prosecutor indicated that the charges were a result of an incident in which Poundstone was driving her children while intoxicated. She accepted a plea agreement and pleaded "no contest" to felony child endangerment and a misdemeanor charge of inflicting injury on a child. In exchange, the three charges of lewd conduct were dropped by prosecutors.

Poundstone was sentenced to five years probation and 180 days in an alcohol rehabilitation program. Following completion of the program, she was granted full custody of her adopted children but permanently lost custody of two other children who were in her home as part of the foster care system. Source (edited): "http://en.wikipedia.org/wiki/Paula_Poundstone"

T. E. Lawrence

Lieutenant Colonel **Thomas Edward Lawrence**, CB, DSO (16 August 1888 – 19 May 1935), known professionally as **T. E. Lawrence**, was a British Army officer renowned especially for his liaison role during the Arab Revolt against Ottoman Turkish rule of 1916–18. The extraordinary breadth and variety of his activities and associations, and his ability to describe them vividly in writing, earned him international fame as **Lawrence of Arabia**, a title which was used for the 1962 film based on his First World War activities.

Lawrence was born illegitimately in Tremadog, Wales in August 1888 to Sir Thomas Chapman and Sarah Junner, a governess, who was herself illegitimate. Chapman left his wife to live with Sarah Junner, and they called themselves Mr and Mrs Lawrence. In the summer of 1896 the Lawrences moved to Oxford, where from 1907 to 1910 young Lawrence studied history at Jesus College, graduating with First Class Honours. He became a practising archaeologist in the Middle East, working with David George Hogarth and Leonard Woolley on various excavations. In January 1914, following the outbreak of the First World War, Lawrence was co-opted by the British military to undertake a military survey of the Negev Desert while doing archaeological research.

Lawrence's public image was due in part to American journalist Lowell Thomas' sensationalised reportage of the revolt as well as to Lawrence's autobiographical account *Seven Pillars of Wisdom* (1922).

Early life

T. E. Lawrence's birthplace, Gorphwysfa, now known as Snowdon Lodge

Lawrence was born on 16 August 1888 in Tremadog, Caernarfonshire (now Gwynedd), Wales, in a house named Gorphwysfa, now known as Snowdon Lodge. His Anglo-Irish father, Thomas Robert Tighe Chapman, who in 1914 inherited the title of seventh Baronet of Westmeath in Ireland, had left his wife Edith for his daughters' governess Sarah Junner. Junner's mother, Elizabeth Junner, had named as Sarah's father a "John Junner - shipwright journeyman", though she had been living as an unmarried servant in the household of a John Lawrence, ship's carpenter, just four months earlier. The couple did not marry but were known as Mr and Mrs Lawrence.

Thomas Chapman and Sarah Junner had five sons born out of wedlock, of whom Thomas Edward was the second eldest. From Wales the family moved to Kirkcudbright in Dumfries and Galloway, then Dinard in Brittany, then to Jersey. From 1894–96 the family lived at Langley Lodge (now demolished), set in private woods between the eastern borders of the New Forest and Southampton Water in Hampshire. Mr Lawrence sailed and took the boys to watch yacht racing in the Solent off Lepe beach. By the time they left, the eight-year-old Ned (as Lawrence became known) had developed a taste for the countryside and outdoor activities.

In the summer of 1896 the Lawrences moved to 2 Polstead Road (now marked with a blue plaque) in Oxford, where, until 1921, they lived under the names of Mr and Mrs Lawrence. Lawrence attended the City of Oxford High School for Boys, where one of the four houses was later named *"Lawrence"* in his honour; the school closed in 1966. As a schoolboy, one of his favourite pastimes was to cycle to country churches and make brass rubbings. Lawrence and one of his brothers became commissioned officers in the Church Lads' Brigade at St Aldate's Church.

Lawrence claimed that in about 1905, he ran away from home and served for a few weeks as a boy soldier with the Royal Garrison Artillery at St Mawes Castle in Cornwall, from which he was bought out. No evidence of this can be found in army records.

Archaeology in the Middle East

From 1907 to 1910 Lawrence studied history at Jesus College, Oxford. During the summers of 1907 and 1908, he toured France by bicycle, collecting photographs, drawings and measurements of castles dating from the mediaeval period. In the summer of 1909, he set out alone on a three-month walking tour of crusader castles in Ottoman Syria, during which he travelled 1,000 mi (1,600 km) on foot. Lawrence graduated with First Class Honours after submitting a thesis entitled *The influence of the Crusades on European Military Architecture – to the end of the 12th century* based on his own field research in France, notably in Châlus, and the Middle East.

Leonard Woolley (*left*) and T.E. Lawrence at Carchemish, ca. 1912

On completing his degree in 1910, Lawrence commenced postgraduate research in mediaeval pottery with a Senior Demy, a form of scholarship, at Magdalen College, Oxford, which he abandoned after he was offered the opportunity to become a practising archaeologist in the Middle East. Lawrence was a polyglot whose published work demonstrates competence in French, Ancient Greek, and Arabic.

T.E. Lawrence and Leonard Woolley (*right*) at Carchemish, spring 1913

In December 1910 he sailed for Beirut, and on arrival went to Jbail (Byblos), where he studied Arabic. He then went to work on the excavations at Carchemish, near Jerablus in northern Syria, where he worked under D. G. Hogarth and R. Campbell-Thompson of the British Museum. He would later state that everything that he had accomplished, he owed to Hogarth. As the site lay near an important crossing on the Baghdad Railway, knowledge gathered there was of considerable importance to the military. While excavating ancient Mesopotamian sites, Lawrence met Gertrude Bell, who was to influence him during his time in the Middle East.

In late 1911, Lawrence returned to England for a brief sojourn. By November he was en route to Beirut for a second season at Carchemish, where he was to work with Leonard Woolley. Prior to resuming work there, however, he briefly worked with Flinders Petrie at Kafr Ammar in Egypt.

Lawrence continued making trips to the Middle East as a field archaeologist until the outbreak of the First World War. In January 1914, Woolley and Lawrence were co-opted by the British military as an archaeological smokescreen for a British military survey of the Negev Desert. They were funded by the Palestine Exploration Fund to search for an area referred to in the Bible as the "Wilderness of Zin"; along the way, they undertook an archaeological survey of the Negev Desert. The Negev was of strategic importance, as it would have to be crossed by any Ottoman army attacking Egypt in the event of war. Woolley and Lawrence subsequently published a report of the expedition's archaeological findings, but a more important result was an updated mapping of the area, with special attention to features of military relevance such as water sources. Lawrence also visited Aqaba and Petra.

From March to May 1914, Lawrence worked again at Carchemish. Following the outbreak of hostilities in August 1914, on the advice of S.F. Newcombe, Lawrence did not immediately enlist in the British Army; he held back until October, when he was commissioned on the General List.

Arab revolt

Lawrence at Rabegh, north of Jidda, 1917

At the outbreak of the First World War Lawrence was a university post-graduate researcher who had for years travelled extensively within the Ottoman Empire provinces of the Levant (Transjordan and Palestine) and Mesopotamia (Syria and Iraq) under his own name. As such he became known to the Turkish Interior Ministry authorities and their German technical advisors. Lawrence came into contact with the Ottoman–German technical advisers, travelling over the German-designed, -built, and -financed railways during the course of his researches.

Even if Lawrence had not volunteered, the British would probably have recruited him for his first-hand knowledge of Syria, the Levant, and Mesopotamia. He was eventually posted to Cairo on the Intelligence Staff of the GOC Middle East.

Contrary to later myth, it was neither Lawrence nor the Army that conceived a campaign of internal insurgency against the Ottoman Empire in the Middle East, but rather the Arab Bureau of Britain's Foreign Office. The Arab Bureau had long felt it likely that a campaign instigated and financed by outside powers, supporting the breakaway-minded tribes and regional challengers to the Turkish government's centralised rule of their empire, would pay great dividends in the diversion of effort that would be needed to meet such a challenge. The Arab Bureau had recognised the strategic value of what is today called the "asymmetry" of such conflict. The Ottoman authorities would have to devote from a hundred to a thousand times the resources to contain the threat of such an internal rebellion compared to the Allies' cost of sponsoring it.

At that point in the Foreign Office's thinking they were not considering the region as candidate territories for incorporation in the British Empire, but only as an extension of the range of British Imperial influence, and the weakening and destruction of a German ally, the Ottoman Empire.

During the war, Lawrence fought with Arab irregular troops under the command of Emir Faisal, a son of Sherif Hussein of Mecca, in extended guerrilla operations against the armed forces of the Ottoman Empire. He persuaded the Arabs not to make a frontal assault on the Ottoman stronghold in Medina but allowed the Turkish army to tie up troops in the city garrison. The Arabs were then free to direct most of their attention to the Turks' weak point, the Hejaz railway that supplied the garrison. This vastly expanded the battlefield and tied up even more Ottoman troops, who were then forced to protect the railway and repair the constant damage.

The capture of Aqaba

Lawrence at Aqaba, 1917

In 1917, Lawrence arranged a joint action with the Arab irregulars and forces under Auda Abu Tayi (until then in the employ of the Ottomans) against the strategically located but lightly defended town of Aqaba. On 6 July, after a surprise overland attack, Aqaba fell to Lawrence and the Arab forces. After Aqaba, Lawrence was promoted to major. Fortunately for Lawrence, the new commander-in-chief of the Egyptian Expeditionary Force, General Sir Edmund Allenby, agreed to his strategy for the revolt, stating after the war:

"I gave him a free hand. His cooperation was marked by the utmost loyalty, and I never had anything but praise for his work, which, indeed, was invaluable throughout the campaign."

Lawrence now held a powerful position, as an adviser to Faisal and a person who had Allenby's confidence.

The fall of Damascus

The following year, Lawrence was involved in the capture of Damascus in the final weeks of the war and was promoted to lieutenant-colonel in 1918. In newly liberated Damascus—which he had envisaged as the capital of an Arab state—Lawrence was instrumental in establishing a provisional Arab government under Faisal. Faisal's rule as king, however, came to an abrupt end in 1920, after the battle of Maysaloun, when the French Forces of General Gouraud under the command of General Mariano Goybet, entered Damascus, breaking Lawrence's dream of an independent Arabia.

As was his habit when travelling before the war, Lawrence adopted many local customs and traditions (many photographs show him in the desert wearing white Arab dishdasha and riding camels).

During the closing years of the war he sought, with mixed success, to convince his superiors in the British government that Arab independence was in their interests. The secret Sykes-Picot Agreement between France and Britain contradicted the promises of independence he had made to the Arabs and frustrated his work.

In 1918 he co-operated with war correspondent Lowell Thomas for a short period. During this time Thomas and his cameraman Harry Chase shot a great deal of film and many photographs, which Thomas used in a highly lucrative film that toured the world after the war.

Post-war years

Emir Faisal's party at Versailles, during the Paris Peace Conference of 1919. Left to right: Rustum Haidar, Nuri as-Said, Prince Faisal (front), Captain Pisani (rear), T. E. Lawrence, Faisal's black slave (name unknown), Captain Hassan Khadri.

Immediately after the war, Lawrence worked for the Foreign Office, attending the Paris Peace Conference between January and May as a member of Faisal's delegation. He served for much of 1921 as an advisor to Winston Churchill at the Colonial Office.

In August 1919, the American journalist Lowell Thomas launched a colorful photo show in London entitled *With Allenby in Palestine* which included a lecture, dancing, and music. Initially, Lawrence played only a supporting role in the show, but when Thomas realized that it was the photos of Lawrence dressed as a Bedouin that had captured the public's imagination, he shot some more photos in London of him in Arab dress. With the new photos, Thomas relaunched his show as *With Allenby in Palestine and Lawrence in Arabia* in early 1920; it was extremely popular. Thomas' shows made Lawrence, who until then been rather obscure, into a household name.

In August 1922, Lawrence enlisted in the Royal Air Force as an aircraftman under the name John Hume Ross. He was soon exposed and, in February 1923, was forced out of the RAF. He changed his name to T. E. Shaw and joined the Royal Tank Corps in 1923. He was unhappy there and repeatedly petitioned to rejoin the RAF, which finally readmitted him in August 1925. A fresh burst of publicity after the publication of *Revolt in the Desert* (see below) resulted in his assignment to a remote base in British India in late 1926, where he remained until the end of 1928. At that time he was forced to return to Britain after rumours began to circulate that he was involved in espionage activities.

Col. T. E. Lawrence, Emir Abdullah, Air Marshal Sir Geoffrey Salmond, Sir Herbert Samuel H.B.M. high commissioner and Sir Wyndham Deedes and others in Jerusalem.

He purchased several small plots of land in Chingford, built a hut and swimming pool there, and visited frequently. This was removed in 1930 when the Chingford Urban District Council acquired the land and passed it to the City of London Corporation, but re-erected the hut in the grounds of The Warren, Loughton, where it remains, neglected, today. Lawrence's tenure of the Chingford land has now been commemorated by a plaque fixed on the sighting obelisk on Pole Hill.

He continued serving in the RAF based at Bridlington, East Riding of Yorkshire, specialising in high-speed boats and professing happiness, and it was with considerable regret that he left the service at the end of his enlistment in March 1935.

Lawrence was a keen motorcyclist, and, at different times, had owned seven Brough Superior motorcycles. His seventh motorcycle is on display at the Imperial War Museum. Among the books Lawrence is known to have carried with him on his military campaigns is Thomas Malory's *Morte D'Arthur*. Accounts of the 1934 discovery of the Winchester Manuscript of the *Morte* include a report that Lawrence followed Eugene Vinaver—a Malory scholar—by motorcycle from Manchester to Winchester upon reading of the discovery in *The Times*.

Death

At the age of 46, two months after leaving the service, Lawrence was fatally injured in an accident on his Brough Superior SS100 motorcycle in Dorset, close to his cottage, Clouds Hill, near Wareham. A dip in the road obstructed his view of two boys on their bicycles; he swerved to avoid them, lost control and was thrown over the handlebars. He died six days later on 19 May 1935. The spot is marked by a small memorial at the side of the road.

The circumstances of Lawrence's death had far-reaching consequences. One of the doctors attending him was the neurosurgeon Hugh Cairns. He was profoundly affected by the incident, and consequently began a long study of what he saw as the unnecessary loss of life by motorcycle dispatch riders through head injuries. His research led to the use of crash helmets by both military and civilian motorcyclists.

Lawrence on a Brough Superior SS100

Moreton Estate, which borders Bovington Camp, was owned by family cousins, the Frampton family. Lawrence had rented and later bought Clouds Hill from the Framptons. He had been a frequent visitor to their home, Okers Wood House, and had for years corresponded with Louisa Frampton. On Lawrence's death, his mother arranged with the Framptons for him to be buried in their family plot at Moreton Church. His coffin was transported on the Frampton estate's bier. Mourners included Winston and Clementine Churchill and Lawrence's youngest brother, Arnold.

A bust of Lawrence was placed in the crypt at St Paul's Cathedral and a stone effigy by Eric Kennington remains in the Anglo-Saxon church of St Martin, Wareham.

Writings

Throughout his life, Lawrence was a prolific writer. A large portion of his output was epistolary; he often sent several letters a day. Several collections of his letters have been published. He corresponded with many notable figures, including George Bernard Shaw, Edward Elgar, Winston Churchill, Robert Graves, Noël Coward, E. M. Forster, Siegfried Sassoon, John Buchan, Augustus John and Henry Williamson. He met Joseph Conrad and commented perceptively on his works. The many letters that he sent to Shaw's wife, Charlotte, offer a revealing side of his character.

In his lifetime, Lawrence published four major texts. Two were translations: Homer's *Odyssey*, and *The Forest Giant* — the latter an otherwise forgotten work of French fiction. He received a flat fee for the second translation, and negotiated a generous fee plus royalties for the first.

Seven Pillars of Wisdom

14 Barton Street, London S.W.1, where Lawrence lived while writing *Seven Pillars*.

Lawrence's major work is *Seven Pillars of Wisdom*, an account of his war experiences. In 1919 he had been elected to a seven-year research fellowship at All Souls College, Oxford, providing him with support while he worked on the book. In addition to being a memoir of his experiences during the war, certain parts also serve as essays on military strategy, Arabian culture and geography, and other topics. Lawrence rewrote *Seven Pillars of Wisdom* three times; once "blind" after he lost the manuscript while changing trains at Reading railway station.

The list of his alleged "embellishments" in *Seven Pillars* is long, though many such allegations have been disproved with time, most definitively in Jeremy Wilson's authorised biography. However Lawrence's own notebooks refute his claim to have crossed the Sinai Peninsula from Aqaba to the Suez Canal in just 49 hours without any sleep. In reality this famous camel ride lasted for more than 70 hours and was interrupted by two long breaks for sleeping which Lawrence omitted when he wrote his book.

Lawrence acknowledged having been helped in the editing of the book by George Bernard Shaw. In the preface to *Seven Pillars*, Lawrence offered his "thanks to Mr. and Mrs. Bernard Shaw for countless suggestions of great value and diversity: and for all the present semicolons."

The first public edition was published in 1926 as a high-priced private subscription edition, printed in London by Roy Manning Pike and Herbert John Hodgson, with illustrations by Eric Kennington, Augustus John, Paul Nash, Blair Hughes-Stanton and his wife Gertrude Hermes. Lawrence was afraid that the public would think that he would make a substantial income from the book, and he stated that it was written as a result of his war service. He vowed not to take any money from it, and indeed he did not, as the sale price was one third of the production costs. This left Lawrence in substantial debt.

Revolt in the Desert

Sketch by Augustus John, 1919

Revolt in the Desert was an abridged version of *Seven Pillars*, which he began in 1926 and was published in March 1927 in both limited and trade editions. He undertook a needed but reluctant publicity exercise, which resulted in a best-seller. Again he vowed not to take any fees from the publication, partly to appease the subscribers to *Seven Pillars* who had paid dearly for their editions. By the fourth reprint in 1927, the debt from *Seven Pillars* was paid off. As Lawrence left for military service in India at the end of 1926, he set up the "Seven Pillars Trust" with his friend D. G. Hogarth as a trustee, in which he made over the copyright and any surplus income of *Revolt in the Desert*. He later told Hogarth that he had "made the Trust final, to save myself the temptation of reviewing it, if *Revolt* turned out a best seller."

The resultant trust paid off the debt, and Lawrence then invoked a clause in his publishing contract to halt publication of the abridgment in the UK. However, he allowed both American editions and translations, which resulted in a substantial flow of income. The trust paid income either into an educational fund for children of RAF officers who lost their lives or were invalided as a result of service, or more substantially into the RAF Benevolent Fund.

Posthumous

Lawrence left unpublished *The Mint*, a memoir of his experiences as an enlisted man in the Royal Air Force. For this, he worked from a notebook that he kept while enlisted, writing of the daily lives of enlisted men and his desire to be a part of something larger than himself: the Royal Air Force. The book is stylistically very different from *Seven Pillars of Wisdom*, using sparse prose as opposed to the complicated syntax found in *Seven Pillars*. It was published posthumously, edited by his brother, Professor A. W. Lawrence.

After Lawrence's death, A. W. Lawrence inherited all Lawrence's estate and his copyrights as the sole beneficiary. To pay the inheritance tax, he sold the U.S. copyright of *Seven Pillars of Wisdom* (subscribers' text) outright to Doubleday Doran in 1935. Doubleday still controls publication rights of this version of the text of *Seven Pillars of Wisdom* in the USA. In 1936 Prof. Lawrence split the remaining assets of the estate, giving Clouds Hill and many copies of less substantial or historical letters to the nation via the National Trust, and then set up two trusts to control interests in T. E. Lawrence's residual copyrights. To the original Seven Pillars Trust, Prof. Lawrence assigned the copyright in *Seven Pillars of Wisdom*, as a result of which it was given its first general publication. To the Letters and Symposium Trust, he assigned the copyright in *The Mint* and all Lawrence's letters, which were subsequently edited and published in the book *T. E. Lawrence by his Friends* (edited by A. W. Lawrence, London, Jonathan Cape, 1937).

A substantial amount of income went

directly to the RAF Benevolent Fund or for archaeological, environmental, or academic projects. The two trusts were amalgamated in 1986 and, on the death of Prof. A. W. Lawrence, the unified trust also acquired all the remaining rights to Lawrence's works that it had not owned, plus rights to all of Prof. Lawrence's works.

Source (edited): "http://en.wikipedia.org/wiki/T._E._Lawrence"

Tim Gunn

Timothy M. "Tim" Gunn (born July 29, 1953) is an American fashion consultant and television personality. He was on the faculty of Parsons The New School for Design from 1982 to 2007 and was chair of fashion design at the school from August 2000 to March 2007, after which he joined Liz Claiborne as its chief creative officer. He is well-known as on-air mentor to designers on the reality television program *Project Runway*. Gunn's popularity on *Project Runway* led to his spin-off show, Bravo's *Tim Gunn's Guide to Style*, as well as his book *A Guide to Quality, Taste and Style*.

Early life

Gunn was born and raised in Washington, D.C. His father, George William Gunn, was an FBI agent during the administration of FBI Director J. Edgar Hoover. Gunn was a champion swimmer throughout high school, and later attended the Corcoran College of Art and Design, receiving a BFA in sculpture.

According to a video Gunn created for the It Gets Better project, he attempted to commit suicide at the age of 17 by swallowing over 100 pills.

Career

Gunn started working at Parsons in 1982 and served as associate dean from 1989–2000, then became chair in August 2000. He was credited with "retooling and invigorating the curriculum for the 21st century."

Gunn began appearing on *Project Runway* during its first season in 2004, and is known for his catchphrases "Talk to me," "This worries me," "Make it work," "Thank you Mood," "Carry on," "Good morning, designers" and "Go, go go!" *Tim Gunn's Guide to Style*, a reality show in which Gunn gives advice to the fashion-challenged, debuted in September 2007 on the Bravo television network.

Gunn also played a version of himself as a reporter for the fictional *Fashion TV* in two episodes of ABC's *Ugly Betty* in February 2007 and later guest starred on *Drop Dead Diva* in August 2009 as himself.

Gunn left Parsons in 2007 and joined Liz Claiborne as the company's chief creative officer in March of that year.

In April 2007, Abrams Image Publishers released Gunn's book *A Guide to Quality, Taste and Style*, co-written with Kate Moloney, cover photo by Markus Klinko & Indrani. While on tour in Palm Springs, California, the nearby city of Palm Desert honored him with an official resolution declaring April 27, 2007 (the day of his visit) "Timothy M. Gunn Day". He was also presented with a certificate by the city of Palm Springs and a plaque by the nearby city of Rancho Mirage in recognition of his career achievements. While promoting the book in the San Francisco Bay Area in May 2007, Gunn joined the judging panel of Project FiveFour 07, to judge gowns designed by 12 students from San Francisco's Fashion Institute of Design & Merchandising. The competition benefited The Princess Project, a Bay Area charity that gives free prom dresses to high school students who can't afford to buy them on their own.

In May 2009, Gunn served as commencement speaker at the Corcoran College of Art and Design, and received an honorary doctorate from the institution.

He makes sporadic appearances on *The Late Late Show with Craig Ferguson's* "Dear Aquaman" segments, helping or standing in for Aquaman (Ferguson), answering letters and dispensing advice.

He guest starred as Barney's personal tailor on the 100th episode of *How I Met Your Mother*.

Gunn is guest-starring as himself on the 6th episode of CW's fourth season of *Gossip Girl*, "Easy J".

In other media

In August 2007, "Tim Gunn's Podcast (a reality chamber opera)" by Jeffrey Lependorf premiered at the Cornelia Street Cafe in New York City. It received its first run one year later at New York International Fringe Festival.

Gunn appeared in a backup story in the first issue of *Models Inc.*, a fashion-themed comic book miniseries published by Marvel Comics that debuted in September 2009 to coincide with New York City's style showcase. Gunn appeared on a variant cover of the issue illustrated by Phil Jimenez. In the series, which is written by *Project Runway* fan Mark Sumerak and illustrated by Jimenez, Gunn dons the Iron Man armor to foil an attack against the New York Fashion Museum.

Gunn appeared in the opening skit on the 62nd Primetime Emmy Awards to style Jimmy Fallon to look like Bruce Springsteen, from his Born in the USA album.

Public critic

Gunn has been a public critic of the fashion taste of several high-profile women, including Meryl Streep, Hillary Clinton, and The Kardashians. In criticizing Clinton, he said, "I think she's confused about what her gender is. She's so mannish in her dress." About Streep, he said that, "I would love to have a chat with Meryl Streep about the semiotics of clothes ... she believes she's too smart for fashion." With regard to the Kardashians, he said, "I just think the Kardashians have an absence of taste and I don't think that that should be perpetuated."

Personal life

Tori Spelling and Gunn co-presenting at an event in November 2007.

Gunn lives in New York City and is openly gay. In a 2006 interview with *Instinct*, Gunn stated that he had not been in a relationship since the early 1980s, following the abrupt end of a six-year relationship, and that he still loves his former partner, though they are not in touch.

Gunn is an outspoken critic of clothing designs using animal fur. In 2008, he narrated a video about rabbit fur farming in China for animal rights group PETA. He termed the treatment of animals used for fur as "egregiously irresponsible".

Filmography

- *Project Runway* (2004–present)
- *Drinks with LX* (2006)
- *Ugly Betty* (2007)
- *Tim Gunn's Guide to Style* (2007–2008)
- *American Dad!* (2008)
- *The Replacements* (2008)
- *Drop Dead Diva* (2009)
- *Project Runway: All-Star Challenge* (2009)
- *The Biggest Loser: Second Chances* (2009)
- *How I Met Your Mother* (2010)
- *Sex and the City 2* (2010)
- *Gossip Girl* (2010)
- *The Smurfs* (2011)

Published works

- Gunn, Tim; Moloney, Kate (2007), *Tim Gunn: A Guide to Quality, Taste & Style*, Harry N. Abrams, Inc., ISBN 0810992841
- Gunn, Tim; Calhoun, Ada (September 2010), *Gunn's Golden Rules: Life's Little Lessons for Making It Work*, Gallery, ISBN 1439176566
- Gunn, Tim (May 2011), *Shaken, Not Stirred*, Tim Gunn, ASIN B004UN4L9E

Source (edited): "http://en.wikipedia.org/wiki/Tim_Gunn"